GUIDELINES

VOL 32 / PART 3
September–December 2016

Commissioned by **David Spriggs**; *Edited by* **Lisa Cherrett**

GW00691778

Guidelines © BRF 2016

The Bible Reading Fellowship
15 The Chambers, Vineyard, Abingdon OX14 3FE
Tel: 01865 319700; Fax: 01865 319701
E-mail: enquiries@brf.org.uk; Websites: www.brf.org.uk; www.biblereadingnotes.org.uk

ISBN 978 0 85746 398 2

Distributed in Australia by Mediacom Education Inc., PO Box 610, Unley, SA 5061.
Tel: 1800 811 311; Fax: 08 8297 8719;
E-mail: admin@mediacom.org.au
Available also from all good Christian bookshops in Australia.
For individual and group subscriptions in Australia:
Mrs Rosemary Morrall, PO Box W35, Wanniassa, ACT 2903.

Distributed in New Zealand by Scripture Union Wholesale, PO Box 760, Wellington
Tel: 04 385 0421; Fax: 04 384 3990; E-mail: suwholesale@clear.net.nz

Publications distributed to more than 60 countries

Acknowledgments

Printed by Gutenberg Press, Tarxien, Malta.

Suggestions for using *Guidelines*

Set aside a regular time and place, if possible, when you can read and pray undisturbed. Before you begin, take time to be still and, if you find it helpful, use the BRF prayer.

In *Guidelines*, the introductory section provides context for the passages or themes to be studied, while the units of comment can be used daily, weekly, or whatever best fits your timetable. You will need a Bible (more than one if you want to compare different translations) as Bible passages are not included. At the end of each week is a 'Guidelines' section, offering further thoughts about, or practical application of what you have been studying.

Occasionally, you may read something in *Guidelines* that you find particularly challenging, even uncomfortable. This is inevitable in a series of notes which draws on a wide spectrum of contributors, and doesn't believe in ducking difficult issues. Indeed, we believe that *Guidelines* readers much prefer thought-provoking material to a bland diet that only confirms what they already think.

If you do disagree with a contributor, you may find it helpful to go through these three steps. First, think about why you feel uncomfortable. Perhaps this is an idea that is new to you, or you are not happy at the way something has been expressed. Or there may be something more substantial—you may feel that the writer is guilty of sweeping generalisation, factual error, theological or ethical misjudgment. Second, pray that God would use this disagreement to teach you more about his word and about yourself. Third, think about what you will do as a result of the disagreement. You might resolve to find out more about the issue, or write to the contributor or the editors of *Guidelines*.

To send feedback, you may email or write to BRF at the addresses shown opposite. If you would like your comment to be included on our website, please email connect@brf.org.uk You can also Tweet to @brfonline; please use the hashtag #brfconnect.

Writers in this issue

Pete Wilcox is Dean of Liverpool and was previously Canon Chancellor at Lichfield Cathedral. He has been in ordained ministry for over 25 years, serving mostly in urban parishes in the north-east and the West Midlands.

David Spriggs has retired from Bible Society but continues his work with them as a consultant. His main role is as a team minister at the Hinckley Baptist Church, with special responsibility to work with the leaders.

Paul Moore is Archdeacon for Mission Development in the Diocese of Winchester. Previously Vicar of St Wilfrid's Church, Cowplain, in Portsmouth Diocese, he was part of a team that created and launched the first Messy Church there in 2004.

Ian Macnair worked in church pastoral ministry, Bible college lecturing and administration before his retirement. His writings include *Teach Yourself New Testament Greek* (Nelson, 1995).

Alec Gilmore, a Baptist minister and a frequent contributor to *Guidelines*, has contributed to many Christian publications in the UK and US and written extensively on Baptist and ecumenical affairs as well as biblical studies.

Antony Billington is Head of Theology at the London Institute for Contemporary Christianity, having formerly taught hermeneutics and biblical theology at London School of Theology.

Hugh Williamson was the Regius Professor of Hebrew at Oxford University until he retired in 2014. He has written extensively on the books of Chronicles, Ezra and Nehemiah, and on Isaiah. He preaches regularly in his home church in Southwold, Suffolk.

Jill Duff is Director of St Mellitus NW (a full-time ordination course in the north-west of England, based at Liverpool Cathedral). Previously, she served as a pioneer minister in Liverpool and taught mission and ecclesiology at Liverpool Hope University. She enjoys being Mum to two boys.

David Kerrigan first joined BMS in 1983 and served in countries including Bangladesh and Sri Lanka, interspersed with periods of study and church leadership in the UK. He has been General Director of BMS World Mission since 2009.

David Spriggs writes...

I have a personal struggle each year, as summer gives way to autumn and we head for the dark nights of December. Of course, if you are in the southern hemisphere your experience is quite different, but for me these months are downhill all the way, from the glory of autumn trees to endless dark and usually grey clouds and rain. Some of our notes in this autumn issue engage with the struggles depicted in the Bible.

The book of Judges tells of increasingly desperate times for God's people and their leaders as they settle in the land of promise but become more and more compromised. Pete Wilcox helps us to enter into this struggle and to see God's light amid the chaos. 2 Corinthians shows us a very different kind of struggle, as Paul wrestles both with the Corinthian Christians, who are tempted to doubt his integrity, and with his own sufferings. Antony Billington helps us to gain clarity about the issues. Our Gospel readings are Luke 9:51—13:35. Here we see Jesus' conflict with those who oppose him and with his disciples' limited understanding. There are also hints about his own struggles as he makes his way towards Jerusalem.

However, there is also much to stimulate and uplift us in these notes. Paul Moore shares the insights he has gleaned about twelve aspects of a fully functioning transformed Christian community. Alec Gilmore adds to our Old Testament diet, creating significant connections for us and our worship with Exodus 25—34, which deals with the tabernacle and associated matters. Hugh Williamson shares his scholarly insights and deep faith as he unpacks a lesser-known part of Isaiah, chapters 13—39; this warrants careful attention and reflection.

Ian Macnair then tackles less familiar New Testament materials, the letters of 2 Peter and Jude. Again we meet Christians under pressure, sometimes from a lack of focused endeavour in their discipleship and sometimes from misleading teaching.

At the end of December, we conclude with two uplifting weeks of study. First, Jill Duff's notes on the spirituality of motherhood, through the experiences of Mary, raise deep issues for us all, whether male or female, mothers or not. Finally, David Kerrigan challenges us about 'mission and incarnation'. His thoughts encompass us all, for the calling of traditional 'missionaries' provides a template that we can apply to mission everywhere.

The BRF Prayer

Almighty God,
you have taught us that your word is a lamp for our
feet and a light for our path. Help us, and all who
prayerfully read your word, to deepen our
fellowship with you and with each other through your love.
And in so doing may we come to know you more fully,
love you more truly, and follow more faithfully in
the steps of your son Jesus Christ, who lives and
reigns with you and the Holy Spirit,
one God for evermore. Amen.

A Prayer for Remembrance

Heavenly Father, we commit ourselves to work in
penitence and faith for reconciliation between the
nations, that all people may, together, live in
freedom, justice and peace. We pray for all who
in bereavement, disability and pain continue to
suffer the consequences of fighting and terror.
We remember with thanksgiving and sorrow those
whose lives, in world wars and conflicts past and
present, have been given and taken away.

FROM AN ORDER OF SERVICE FOR REMEMBRANCE SUNDAY,
CHURCHES TOGETHER IN BRITAIN AND IRELAND 2005

Judges

The book of Judges is among the most lurid and gruesome in the Bible, yet it remains a favourite with children in Sunday school. Where would we be without Samson and Gideon? It is also among the most misunderstood books in the Bible: careful readers quickly see that its heroes are deeply flawed. To a man (Deborah is the odd one out, in terms of both her gender and her integrity), 'the judges' participate in the sins of their people. But perhaps the text is making just this point: in the deliverance of sinners, God has always been prepared to choose and use sinners. Christians understand this well: apart from Jesus, sinners are the only people available.

The title 'the Judges' places the book in historical context. It is set in the time between the conquest of Canaan and the rise of King Saul. The opening and closing verses make these limits explicit: it is the period after the death of Joshua (1:1) and before there was any 'king in Israel' (21:25). But the title 'the Judges' may also mislead us if it conjures up a court of law. In our story, the judges are not those who ensure justice; they are deliverers who rescue their people from their enemies. Indeed, in this book the title 'judge' is only once applied to an individual—in 11:27, where the referent is God.

The book of Judges has a clear structure, falling into three parts. There's an introduction, 1:1—3:6, which sets out the causes of the troubles in the book; then a middle section, 3:7—16:31, in which cycles of trouble are described and individual 'judges' feature strongly; and a final section, 17:1—21:25, in which we hear the outcome of these troubles.

The main theme of the book is the 'paganisation' of Israel. Rescued by God from slavery in Egypt, called into covenant relationship with God and brought dramatically, by conquest, into the promised land, Israel settles down to life as a free people. That is the point to which the first six books of the Bible bring us. The book of Judges then picks up the story of Israel's failure to live as God's holy people as the nation capitulates instead to the culture of the Canaanites. The result is moral and social chaos.

Bible quotations are taken from the New Revised Standard Version.

1 The fundamental problem for Israel

Judges 1:1–4, 8–32

Christians are often slow to appreciate that while holy scripture is, of course, always more than carefully crafted literature, it is seldom less than that. The book of Judges illustrates this neatly, and the very first chapter of the book is a case in point.

Judges 1 looks like a fairly unpromising text at first sight. It appears to be a repetitive inventory, charting Israel's mixed progress in taking possession of the promised land after the death of Joshua, relieved by a few rather random anecdotes; but in fact the passage traces a steady decline.

Judah, charged by the Lord with taking the lead in the fight against the Canaanites, enjoys considerable success in the first half of the chapter. Victory at Bezek (v. 4) is followed by victory against Jerusalem (v. 8), Hebron (v. 10), Debir (v. 11), Zephath (v. 17) and, finally, Gaza, Ashkelon and Ekron (v. 18), but even Judah does not have everything his own way. Verse 19 sounds the first note of trouble: even though 'the Lord was with Judah... [he] could not drive out the inhabitants of the plain, because they had chariots of iron'.

What Judah 'could' not do, the remaining tribes 'did' not do. Benjamin 'did not drive out the Jebusites' (v. 21); although 'the Lord was with' the house of Joseph (v. 22), Manasseh 'did not drive out the inhabitants of Beth-shean' (v. 27) and Ephraim 'did not drive out the Canaanites who lived in Gezer' (v. 29). Simple notes record failure on the part of Zebulun, Asher and Naphtali, but the nadir is reserved for Dan, in conclusion. With Dan, it is not merely a failure to drive out the resident tribes: they found themselves driven back by the Amorites. The further north the Israelites took the battle, the less fully they were able to occupy the land.

Observant readers will note the absence of any reference to Gad and Reuben (whose tribal allotments were east of the Jordan) and Levi (which had no allotment of land). References to Simeon in alliance with Judah (in verses 3 and 17) are easily missed, but it is hard to account for the absence of any reference to Issachar.

While Christian readers rightly flinch at the assertion that the people of Judah 'put [Jerusalem] to the sword and set the city on fire' (v. 8) and even 'devoted [Zephath] to destruction' (v. 17), the theological commitment of the writer of this text is clear: the failure to drive out the Canaanites sowed seeds of trouble, which the Israelites would later reap bitterly.

2 Cyclical literary markers set out

Judges 2:7–19; 3:7–11

The death of Joshua and his contemporaries not only created a leadership crisis for Israel; apparently it also deprived Israel of its capacity to remember the Lord and his work. As a result, Israel fell repeatedly into idolatry.

In verses 10–19, the author of Judges introduces a six-part cycle, elements of which recur programmatically in the narratives that dominate the central section of the book (3:7—16:31):

- The Israelites did what was evil in the sight of the Lord (v. 11) (rebellion).
- The anger of the Lord was kindled against the Israelites, and he sold them into the power of their enemies (v. 14) (retribution).
- The Israelites were in great distress and cried out to the Lord (v. 15) (repentance).
- The Lord raised up judges (v. 16) (raised up).
- The Lord delivered the Israelites from the hand of their enemies (v. 18) (rescue).
- The judge died and the people relapsed (v. 19) (relapse).

All six elements of this cycle will be made explicit in the account of the first 'major' judge, Othniel, despite the account's brevity (cycle one, 3:7–11). In fact, strip out the formulae and not much remains of the story. But this is the only occasion when all six elements feature so neatly. In relation to the remaining five major judges, the pattern is one of decline: the elements of the cycle are stated with dwindling frequency. So, in the case of Ehud (3:12–30), the deliverance of Israel is only implied (by the report in verse 30 that 'Moab was subdued'), and the notice of Ehud's death is missing. With regard to the next three judges (Deborah in chapters 4—5, Gideon in chapters 6—8, and Jephthah in chapters 10—12), only the first three elements are explicit at the start of each narrative—although the deliverance of Israel is clearly implied in each case, and it is said of Deborah (5:31) and Gideon (8:28), as it had been of Othniel (3:11) and Ehud (3:30), that on account of their actions 'the land had rest'.

This increasingly patchy application of the cycle is apparently deliberate and reaches its climax in the story of Samson: in his case alone, only the first two elements are listed (13:1). The cycle turns out to be a disintegrating spiral, a reflection perhaps of Israel's sin.

3 Cycle 2: Ehud the left-handed assassin

Judges 3:12–30

The story of Ehud is the first extended narrative in the book of Judges. It's a colourful tale, with plenty of satirical humour and no shortage of gory detail.

Ehud was a Benjaminite—a member of the most junior tribe in Israel—and, though his tribal name meant 'son of my right hand', he was a left-handed man. (If Judges 20:16 is anything to go by, he was evidently in good company among his tribesmen.) In the culture of the Middle East, the left hand is stigmatised: it is the inferior hand, used for dirty work. (Even in English, the word 'sinister' is derived from the Latin for 'left', as 'dextrous' is derived from the Latin for 'right'.)

In Ehud's experience, however, his left-handedness was far from being a liability. It became precisely the means by which he was able to deceive King Eglon and kill him. The text specifies that he used a dagger strapped to his right thigh (v. 21); only a left-handed man would find that arrangement convenient. Ehud thus establishes a pattern among the major judges: humanly (or, in this case, culturally) speaking, each of them has an obvious weakness or failing, yet by God's grace this very thing becomes their strength.

Charged with presenting tribute to Israel's oppressor, Ehud presented a secret matter (v. 19) as well—a matter from God (v. 20). The Hebrew *debar* is ambiguous in this context: although it can mean 'a word' or 'a message' (as in NRSV), it can also mean 'a thing' or even 'a deed'. Ehud's deception is scrupulously honest!

The sequel is undoubtedly intended to make the reader chuckle. The assassination has taken place in Eglon's private chambers, where there is a facility for him to relieve himself. When their master fails to emerge after Ehud's departure, his guards assume, as Ehud intended that they should, that he has taken to his toilet. Since the text has stated bluntly that the dagger-blow emptied Eglon's stomach so that 'the dirt came out' (v. 22), presumably the smell served to confirm the guards in their conclusion. They waited to the point of embarrassment, and, by the time they had worked out that something must be wrong, Ehud had escaped scot-free.

The incident was, in fact, only a beginning. The Israelites subsequently took to the battlefield with Ehud at their head. 'Follow after me,' he said—adding with startling self-effacement, 'the Lord has given your enemies the Moabites into your hand' (v. 28).

4 Cycle 3: Deborah and the role of women

Judges 4

The narratives of the six major judges grow successively longer: Othniel's story is shortest (3:7–11), followed by Ehud's (vv. 12–30). Deborah's story takes up two chapters (4—5), and Gideon's three (6—8). Jephthah's story is admittedly shorter (less than two chapters, 11:1—12:7), but, at four chapters (13—16), Samson's is the longest. As the stories get longer, the judges become more morally flawed. Ehud is presented as a far more noble character than Gideon. There may be a similar trend at work in these stories as far as the female characters are concerned. Deborah and Jael in chapter 4 are much more admirable than Delilah in chapter 16, they are also more heroic and decisive than Jephthah's daughter in chapter 11 and Samson's mother in chapters 13 and 14.

The story of Deborah is introduced without fuss. There is no sense in the text that it is surprising for a woman to exercise the office of either prophetess or judge, but her gender becomes a crucial part of the story.

Speaking both as prophetess and judge, Deborah summons Barak son of Abinoam and commissions him to lead an army of his fellow tribesmen against the Canaanites. It is not clear whether Barak is already an established military leader (Israel's commander-in-chief, equivalent to Sisera on the Canaanite side?) or a novice to whom this calling has come, as it were, out of the blue. He seems to prevaricate: he will accept the commission only if Deborah goes with him. When Deborah agrees, but immediately tells him that 'the road on which [he] is going will not lead to [his] glory' because 'the Lord will sell Sisera into the hand of a woman' (v. 9), there seems to be some censure implied.

Barak wins the battle when the Lord throws Sisera and his army into a panic (v. 15; the commentary provided in 5:20–21 suggests that a cloud-burst might have been involved), but Sisera duly meets his grisly end at the hands not of Barak or any Israelite man but of Jael, a Kenite woman. The violence of her action is only reinforced in the concluding stanzas of the song that follows (5:24–31). The so-called 'Song of Deborah' in Judges 5 (actually sung by Barak too, as verse 1 makes clear) has echoes of the Song of Moses in Exodus 15, and of Psalm 68.

5 Cycle 4: Gideon: the call of a fearful man

Judges 6:11–27, 36–40

The book of Judges is full of irony, and the call of Gideon is an excellent example. When the angel of the Lord appears to our hero, he greets him with the words, 'The Lord is with you, you mighty warrior' (v. 12), and commissions him to 'go in this might of yours and deliver Israel from the hand of Midian' (v. 14). The reader is inclined to laugh out loud. In truth, Gideon is anything but a mighty warrior. He knows this about himself and seeks to tell the angel so (v. 15). His timidity and his need for constant reassurance are key features of Gideon's story.

The fact that his first encounter with the angel of the Lord takes place in a wine press, where Gideon is beating out wheat 'to hide it from the Midianites', may already hint at this timidity: hiding from the enemy is hardly the mark of a macho man. But Gideon's fearfulness is stated unequivocally in verse 27: 'Because he was too afraid of his family and the townspeople to do [as the Lord had told him] by day, he did it by night.' By then (more conventionally) the Lord has already spoken to tell him, 'Do not fear' (v. 23), so it comes as no surprise to find the Lord making a further concession to Gideon's trepidation later in the story (7:10–11).

Similarly, Gideon (rather in the mould of Moses in Exodus 3 and 4) demands signs that he really can rely on the word of the Lord, and the Lord is gracious in providing them (vv. 17–21, 36–40). It seems Gideon himself is aware that he is pushing his luck when he seeks confirmation that God really will do as he has said and deliver Israel through Gideon, by laying out his fleece not once but twice (v. 39). As in the call of Moses, however, it seems to be precisely this sense of inadequacy that makes Gideon an appropriate servant of the Lord. Later we see the Lord whittling down Gideon's army from 32,000 to 300 men and making as much use of their trumpets and torches as their swords (7:2–8, 20): the weaker the vehicle, the clearer it is that the victory belongs to the Lord.

6 Cycle 4: Gideon: the idolatry of the judge

Judges 8:22–35

The sad end to the Gideon story marks a new departure in the Judges story as, for the first time, we encounter a negative value judgement made by the narrator. It is clear that this judge participates in the sinfulness of the people of Israel: the deliverer requires deliverance.

It is possible that the reader is meant to infer a criticism of Gideon earlier, in chapter 7. Before the attack on the Midianites, the Lord painstakingly explains to our hero the rationale for the whittling down of the Israelite army: 'The troops with you are too many for me to give the Midianites into their hand. Israel would only take the credit away from me, saying, "My own hand has delivered me"' (7:2). The Lord means the glory to be exclusively his own, but, in the event, Gideon secures a share in the glory for himself. On the eve of the battle, he instructs his 300 men, 'When I blow the trumpet, I and all who are with me, then you also blow the trumpets around the whole camp, and shout, "For the Lord and for Gideon!"' (7:18).

In his handling of the Ephraimites' complaint in 8:1–3, there is just a brief glimpse of Gideon the statesman, acting wisely and generously. Again, when the Israelites take the initiative and approach Gideon with the request that he should rule over them and establish a dynasty, it is a welcome thing to hear the judge remind the people that the Lord is their king (v. 23). If that is the high point of Gideon's career, however, his fall from grace comes swiftly.

The collecting of golden earrings (vv. 24–25), with a view to melting them down and making something new out of them, might ring an alarm bell for the reader: that was how Aaron's golden calf began (Exodus 32:2–3). The making of an ephod is not obviously an act of spiritual treachery, but, arguably, nor was the making of a golden calf: Aaron apparently intended a faithful festival 'to the Lord' (Exodus 32:5). But just as that proved to be a tragically misguided step, so is this. Predictably, in the context of their susceptibility to idolatry, what might have been a vehicle of true worship becomes the focus of Israel's prostitution, and a snare (v. 27; see 2:3) to Gideon and his family.

Guidelines

Already it is clear that the major judges were a motley crew. Othniel might seem to have been a first-class role model, but we know very little about him. Ehud was presumably to some extent stigmatised by his left-handedness, and Deborah's remarkable career flourished despite her gender. She was undoubtedly a woman who pursued her vocation in a man's world. In the case of Gideon, as we have seen, character flaws became a frank part of the portrait of the judge.

What does this tell us about the grace of God and about the expectations we might appropriately have of our leaders? How does it change the way we think about ourselves and our own vocation, and how might it change the way we pray for those who lead us?

Israel, meanwhile, demonstrates a persistent vulnerability to unfaithfulness. The people seem incapable of anything other than brief episodes of fidelity to their covenant God. What lesson do you think the writer of Judges intends us to derive from this presentation? What expectations do we have of the church (the local congregation and the national institution) in terms of its capacity to live out its calling in faith and love?

12–18 September

1 Abimelech, first king over the Israelites

Judges 9:1–21

After the first four 'major judge' cycles (Othniel, Ehud, Deborah and Gideon) comes a regal interlude.

When the Israelites petitioned Gideon to rule over them (and his son and grandson after him), he deflected them with an apparently godly refusal: 'I will not rule over you, and my son will not rule over you; the Lord will rule over you' (8:23). Yet either this rebuttal was insincere or Gideon changed his mind. He fathered a son to whom he gave the name Abimelech, which means something perilously like 'my father is king' or 'father of a king'. Gideon harboured dynastic ambitions after all.

Certainly, after his father died, Abimelech had no qualms about seizing the kingship by arranging the slaughter of Gideon's other sons (9:5). The survivor, Jotham, foresaw (as the prophet Samuel would also foresee, in 1 Samuel 8:10–18) that the experience of monarchy would not be a happy one for Israel. It would correspond more to the prickliness of the bramble than to the fruitfulness of the olive, the fig or the vine. So it proved: in the rest of Judges 9 we hear how Abimelech fell out with the elders of Shechem (who had earlier supported his bid for power), leading to a terrible loss of life among non-combatants as well as soldiers (9:22–49).

Abimelech's reign lasted only three years, and at the end of that time he laid siege to the city of Thebez (9:50). We don't learn why, perhaps it was just expected of kings that they should always be laying siege here or there. In contemporary politics, after all, it can often appear as if a national leader is not succeeding unless it is at the expense of a neighbour. In the course of this particular siege, however, Abimelech was struck on the head with a millstone by accident (unless it was an act of divine providence) (9:53). Abimelech does not come out of this episode at all well: 'Thus God repaid [him] for the crime he committed against his father in killing his seventy brothers' (9:56). But nor does the city of Shechem, his first ally: 'God also made all the wickedness of the people of Shechem fall back on their heads' (9:57). The only person to come out of the story with credit is Jotham (9:57), but of him nothing further is heard.

2 Cycle 5: Jephthah and the folly of his vow

Judges 11:30–40

Unlike Gideon, Jephthah really was a mighty warrior (see 11:1–3). In living as an outlaw and gathering a motley crew about him, he was a proto-David (see 1 Samuel 22:1–2). He was evidently also something of a wheeler-dealer, a man used to getting his own way, who did not take kindly to being thwarted and had great confidence in his own bargaining ability.

Three times in this chapter we find him in negotiation. The first time (vv. 4–11), it is with the elders of Gilead, who want to make Jephthah their leader. Agreement is reached and the outcome is clearly a happy one from Jephthah's point of view: he becomes their leader. The second time (vv. 12–28), it is with the king of the Ammonites. This time, agreement is not reached, but the text suggests that this outcome, too, was what Jephthah intended. On this occasion, the diplomatic effort was a ruse: Jephthah's intention was to pick a fight. Sure enough, battle followed (vv. 32–33) and the Ammonites were defeated.

The third 'negotiation' (vv. 30–31) is a vow that Jephthah makes to the Lord. Two things set this third example apart from the earlier two. Firstly, whereas those were genuine dialogues, in which the Gileadites and Ammonites played a full part, on this occasion only Jephthah speaks. The Lord remains ominously silent both at the time and in the sequel (see vv. 24–40). Secondly, whereas Jephthah's bargaining skills stood him in good stead in the previous situations, in this case his oath turns out disastrously for him and his family.

It is Jephthah who, alone in this book, has the intuition that 'the Lord is judge' (11:27), and the Spirit of the Lord comes upon him (v. 29), as it came upon Gideon before him (6:34) and will later come upon Samson (13:25; 14:6, 19; 15:14). Ultimately, though, neither his insight into the Lord's status nor his experience of the Spirit prevents his daughter from becoming the victim of his recklessness.

A new depth of disaster follows for Israel at the end of Jephthah's tenure as judge—civil war. The men of Gilead fight and rout the men of Ephraim, with 42,000 casualties on one side alone (12:6).

3 Cycle 6: Samson: a weakness exposed

Judges 14:1–19

Samson's story, the sixth and final 'cycle' among the judges, is extreme. It is the longest story and the only one with a birth narrative attached. It is also the one in which the character of the judge is most fully and most negatively portrayed. Whatever else Samson is, he is not a role model for covenant righteousness and faith.

Judges 13 tells the story of Samson's birth, after the appearance to his mother, the wife of Manoah, of the angel of the Lord. Judges 14 tells us what then 'went down'. The Hebrew verb *yarad* is found five times in this chapter (vv. 1, 5, 7, 10, 19), all at points of transition in the story, thus dividing the narrative into five scenes. Samson 'goes down' to Timnah; his parents 'go down' there with him; Samson 'goes down' to the Philistine woman; his father 'goes down' to her too; and finally Samson 'goes down' to Ashkelon.

Meanwhile, the narrative revolves around who tells what to whom. The Hebrew verb *higgid*, 'to tell' (in this chapter sometimes translated 'to explain'), occurs once in each of the first, second, third and fifth scenes—but ten times in the fourth scene (vv. 10–18, easily the longest).

Samson is a Nazirite, separated to God from birth, because 'it is he who shall begin to deliver Israel from… the Philistines' (13:5), yet it is a Philistine woman whom Samson 'sees' and desires as his wife (14:1–2). We might have wished that his parents had challenged him harder about this, in the light of his calling, but it turns out that 'this was from the Lord; for he was seeking a pretext to act against the Philistines' (v. 4).

Twice, Samson is endued with superhuman strength as the Spirit of the Lord comes upon him. The first time is in the second scene of the story, when he is going to see his future wife in Timnah in the company of his mother and father. He doesn't tell them about the incident but, when a lion attacks him, he kills it with his bare hands. This sets up the riddle that Samson poses to his companions in the fourth and longest scene in the story (vv. 10–18). It is in resolving the narrative (after the cunning of his 30 companions and the disloyalty of his wife) that the Spirit comes upon Samson the second time: he kills 30 Philistines, and the deliverance of the Israelites has begun.

4 Cycle 6: Samson: a weakness exploited

Judges 16

Samson was not one to learn from his mistakes. In this story, as in the previous one, he eventually divulges a secret to his lover on account of her persistent nagging—and in particular because she accuses him of not really loving her (v. 15; compare 14:16).

Judges 16 falls into three parts: it begins and ends with episodes set in Gaza, while the action in the central section is set in Sorek. The first part (vv. 1–3) is a cameo that further underlines Samson's extraordinary strength and the vain attempts of the Philistines to capture him (compare 15:9–17). If it is unworthy of a Nazirite to visit a prostitute (as, within the wider scriptural context, it surely is), the text maintains a discreet silence about it.

Delilah is the only one of the three women who partner Samson in Judges 13—16 to be named, but, like the others, she is a Philistine, and her loyalty to her people is greater than her loyalty to Samson. Even though she acts three times on the misinformation he provides, it seems not to have occurred to Samson that he might be in real danger if he eventually discloses the truth. When he finally confides in Delilah (v. 17), it is the first reference to his Nazirite status and to the razor since 13:5. Even that verse, however, did not make it clear that his hair is such a symbol of his consecration to God that if he is shorn of it, he will also be shorn of his strength. Abandoning his vow (or enabling Delilah to violate it), he is abandoned by God (v. 20).

Gaza, the scene of his earlier triumph, becomes briefly the scene of his humiliation and then of his final vindication. It is undoubtedly careless of his Philistine captors to allow his hair to grow again, but perhaps what is really growing in prison is Samson's sense of himself in relationship to the God to whom he was dedicated at birth. Whatever is meant by the statement in verse 20 that the Lord has left him, it does not prevent the Lord hearing Samson's cry, even though he cries out from within the temple of Dagon.

Samson is not only the last of the judges of Israel and the one whose story is told at greatest length; in what appears to be a tribute, a mark of honour, he is also the only one whose length of tenure is recorded twice (15:20; 16:31).

5 Micah and the Levite

Judges 17—21 is an epilogue. There are no more stories in these chapters about individuals who 'judged Israel' and no more formula-phrases indicating the cycle of rebellion, retribution, repentance, rescue and relapse that constitutes the framework for chapters 3—16.

These five chapters are a unit in their own right, held together by a new refrain: 'in those days, there was no king in Israel.' We meet the refrain four times in all, in 17:6; 18:1; 19:1 and, finally, 21:25 (the very last verse of the book), where it sounds ominously like an epitaph. Israel is in a state of anarchy, and order will not be restored until Samuel anoints King Saul. In the meantime, the two stories in these five chapters illustrate the chaos and depravity that follow when there is no effective leadership in society. Both stories concern Levites in the north of Israel.

Judges 17—18 tells the sad story of a man called Micah, who hires a Levite as a family priest—albeit in a family shrine occupied by a home-made idol. There is a vestige here of the worship of the Lord, but in a very degenerate form. Micah's mother invokes the name of the Lord even in the act of making an idol (17:3). Perhaps there is a clue here to the integrity of the Levite: if he is prepared to serve at an idol-shrine, it should not surprise us that he leaves when a better offer is made, colluding with the theft of his master's possessions. Why should he be a simple domestic priest when he can have the status of serving an entire tribe? (18:19–20). By this point he has, in any case, pronounced God's blessing on the raid that the men of Dan are undertaking (18:6).

The sting in the tail of this story comes in the penultimate verse of chapter 18. It turns out that the Levite, unnamed until this late stage, is none other than Jonathan, son of Gershom, son of Moses. It's an indication of just how far the covenant people of God have strayed from the worship of the living God that Moses' own grandson, a close relative of Aaron, should be capable of such idolatry and disloyalty. But this is what happens when there is no king in Israel.

6 Israel and Benjamin

Judges 21

In the first of the two stories that make up Judges 17—21, there is plenty to deplore. There is idolatry, theft and disloyalty—but there is little violence. The same cannot be said of the final episode of a book not short of gruesome passages. Judges 19—21 is perhaps the most X-rated narrative in the whole Bible.

Like the tale in chapters 17—18, the final story in the book of Judges is about a Levite—a Levite and his concubine. It is also a story about tribal relations in Israel, and about attempts to maintain social order when anarchy threatens. The story breaks into three parts, which correspond to the three chapters, 19—21. If the first is the most brutal, it is also local: the terrible violence perpetrated against the concubine, while viciously executed and graphically described, is nevertheless an act of violence perpetrated against one individual. In chapter 20, the violence spreads: the rest of the tribes of Israel unite against Benjamin, to exact vengeance for the crime that chapter 19 has documented. Upwards of 83,000 are slaughtered in the battles that follow.

The final chapter of Judges is the last instalment in a sorry saga, in which a belated and misguided attempt is made to restore Benjamin to good standing in Israel. In the course of this chapter, which is intended to be a story of reconciliation, thousands more are killed, and hundreds of innocent young women are abducted, first in Jabesh-Gilead and then in Shiloh.

Israel has travelled a long way since the opening chapter of the book, but not in the right direction. The longed-for promised land has become a place of depravity, idolatry and extreme violence. The final sentence is both an indictment of Israel and a pointer to a brighter future: 'In those days there was no king in Israel; all the people did what was right in their own eyes.' At least a few times in the following centuries, Israel would know the blessing of a king worthy of the covenant God, and the social order that a godly ruler can bring.

Guidelines

Judges 9 (the story of Abimelech) is the only chapter in which the Almighty is consistently described as 'God' (vv. 7, 23, 56–57). Elsewhere in Judges, the dominant usage is 'the Lord' (that is, Yahweh, the covenant God, as in Exodus 3:14–15). What are we to make of this correlation? Is some withdrawal of covenant relationship implied, some distancing from the experiment in kingship on the part of 'the Lord'?

It is basically true that in the course of chapters 3—16 the stories about the major judges get longer but also more tawdry, as the judges themselves become less and less helpful as role models for godliness. What are we to make of this trend? How do you understand the Lord's continued commitment not just to Israel but to these individuals, in the light of this trend?

Judges 19 is arguably the most appalling and ghastly chapter in holy scripture. It is also the only chapter of the book in which there is not a single reference to God. What are we to make of this correlation? Is there no room for God in a story so horrible? Does the violence somehow deny his presence?

At the start of the book, the tribes of Israel are united. Later, and until near the end of the book, they are not only disunited but (in chapters 9, 12 and 20) at war with one another. But the final chapter, however misguided, appears to be an attempt by the majority to bring Benjamin back into 'communion'. Is the grace of God at work here?

FURTHER READING

D.I. Block, *Judges, Ruth*, Broadman & Holman, 1999

D.R. Davis, *Judges: Such a great salvation*, Christian Focus, 2000

L.R. Klein, *The Triumph of Irony in the Book of Judges*, Almond Press, 1988

K. Lawson Younger Jr, *Judges, Ruth*, Zondervan 2002

B. Webb, *The Book of Judges*, Eerdmans, 2012

Luke 9:51—13:35

The previous section of Luke's Gospel included the observation, '[The disciples] did not understand this saying… And they were afraid to ask [Jesus] about this saying' (9:45)—the saying being that the Son of Man was going to be betrayed. They failed to understand even though Jesus had commanded them, 'Let these words sink into your ears' (v. 44).

The section we will study over the next three weeks ends with Jesus lamenting over Jerusalem. Before that, we will travel as a disciple with Jesus, learning what it means to be his follower. Much of the material in Matthew's 'Sermon on the Mount' (Matthew 5—7) is here, sketching out the quality of life required for Jesus' disciples. This teaching includes the Lord's Prayer, as well as exhortations to persevere in prayer, avoid anxiety, keep our light shining and enter through the narrow door. At the same time, there are passages that are particular to Luke's Gospel, such as the mission of 'the Seventy' (with instructions on how to deal with the responses), the world-famous parable of the good Samaritan and the cameo conversation between Martha and Jesus. Even when his material is shared with Matthew, Luke often presents it in a different and, arguably, more lively context. So the need to persevere in prayer here follows the memorable parable about the widow and the unresponsive judge, and the teaching about not being anxious follows the humorous but devastating parable about the wealthy and ambitious farmer whom God calls to account.

While there is much to make us smile as we journey with Jesus, controversy, conflict and the shadow of the cross are never far away. The accusation that Jesus works in liaison with Beelzebub indicates this continuing conflict, as does Jesus' acerbic analysis of the behaviour of the Pharisees and teachers of the law. Indeed, the only 'miracle story', in which Jesus heals a woman, is a further sign of the growing tensions that will lead to his condemnation.

Jesus laments that Jerusalem 'kills the prophets and stones those who are sent to it' (13:34), but at the heart of this section is the warning that a similar fate awaits his disciples, with the challenge to be prepared to publicly acknowledge their allegiance to Jesus (12:8–12).

Bible quotations are taken from the New Revised Standard Version.

1 Lack of understanding

Luke 9:51–62

In order to make good sense of this passage, it is helpful to refer to the preceding verses (9:46–50). We then see that it is the final story in a series of three that amplify the lack of perception among the disciples of Jesus.

First (vv. 46–48) the disciples argue about who is the greatest. Jesus seeks to explain the nature of the kingdom by showing them a child—not as an example of those who enter the kingdom of God, but as a sign of how to treat others, because even a child carries the same significance as Jesus himself.

The second story (vv. 49–50) shows the disciples' concern for protectionism, as John tells Jesus that they have tried to stop someone casting out demons in Jesus' name. Did the disciples' action stem from jealousy that this man was doing what they had failed to do (9:40), or was it genuinely seeking to protect the 'Jesus brand', as the person was not a recognised disciple? Again, Jesus expresses a genuine open-heartedness.

Our passage begins by relating the disciples' response when they are refused hospitality by Samaritans, not because of the general antagonism between Jews and Samaritans but 'because his face was set towards Jerusalem' (v. 53). From the Samaritan perspective, Jerusalem was the wrong centre for worship. For us as modern-day readers, the rejection is intensified by the knowledge that Jesus was going there to suffer. For the disciples, it was an anger-provoking snub, and they had been instructed by Jesus himself to reject those who rejected them (9:5). So James and John think they are exercising faith—believing they can call down fire, just as Elijah did. For Jesus, though, this response shows their continuing lack of perception as well as their prejudice (see Luke 10:28–37).

These three instances of a lack of understanding by the current disciples are followed by three cases in which potential disciples also misunderstand the 'cost of discipleship'. Jesus' first response relates to the 'Son of Man' (v. 58) and the next two to the kingdom of God (vv. 60, 62). These references lead in an orderly way to the sending out of the

Seventy who prepare for the coming of the Son of Man and announce the proximity of the kingdom of God.

2 Seventy

Luke 10:1–12

It's well known that this passage is unique to Luke's Gospel. In several respects, it is similar to the sending of the Twelve in Matthew 10:5–15 and Mark 6:7–13, but Luke has his own version of that story too (see 9:1–6). The reference to Sodom in Luke 10:12 (the sending of the Seventy) is not included in Luke's version of the Twelve, but does appear in Matthew's (Matthew 10:15). Is Luke (or his sources) simply inventing another story? Luke does not usually offer us 'duplicate accounts'; this is more frequent in Matthew, who, for instance, has Jesus healing two pairs of blind men (9:27–31; 20:29–34) and gives two accounts of miraculous feedings (Matthew 14:13–21; 15:32–39), as indeed does Mark (6:30–44; 8:1–10).

So what is Luke doing here? In the reference to 'seventy', some scholars have seen a link to the 'seventy elders' whom Moses appointed to help him share the load of leadership (Numbers 11:16–17), but that doesn't take us very far. Is it perhaps a reference to the tradition that 70 Jewish scholars worked on the translation of the Hebrew scriptures into Greek (the Septuagint), thus making it available to Greek readers such as Luke and Theophilus? This seems a rather obscure connection.

Others recognise the tradition that there were 70 nations and suggest, therefore, a link with the mission to the Gentiles in the book of Acts. However, as there is no indication that the Seventy went even to the Samaritans, or that seventy were sent out after Pentecost, it is hard to sustain this suggestion. The only possible indication that these missions by Jesus' disciples might be presenting a model for the early church is the reference to Paul and Barnabas shaking the dust off their feet in Acts 13:51 (compare Luke 10:11; Matthew 10:14).

We can note that between Luke's two stories of the sending of Twelve and Seventy, we read the pivotal account of Jesus' transfiguration (9:28–36). What the story of the Seventy enables Luke to do is to underline that the mission to heal and announce the proximity of the kingdom of God continues even after the transfiguration. The coming crucifixion (Jesus' 'departure', 9:31) in no way lessens the need for mission; indeed, it makes mission more urgent.

3 How will it turn out?

Luke 10:13–20

The first verses of this passage heighten the suspense: how is the mission of the Seventy going to turn out? Jesus utters words of doom for those cities that fail to respond with repentance—that is, preparation for the coming kingdom of God. In Matthew 11:20–24, these words relate to the rejection of Jesus' own work (Matthew 11:20). In Luke, they are placed between the sending and the return of the Seventy and are used to emphasise the continuity between those who go in Jesus' name and Jesus himself. Indeed, we need to read them as part of the address of Jesus to the Seventy, because verse 16 is addressed to them: 'Whoever listens to you, listens to me, and whoever rejects you rejects me, and whoever rejects me rejects him who sent me.'

In addition to sounding remarkably like a verse from John's Gospel, these words prepare the disciples for a very tough assignment. The second half of the reading, though, reports precisely the opposite of what might be expected: 'Even the demons submit to us' (v. 17). This is noteworthy because Jesus' charge to the Seventy made no mention of casting out demons, only to curing the sick (10:9); furthermore, the demons had not submitted to the disciples before (9:40). Even that which proved so difficult for them previously, they have now accomplished 'in your name'.

Their success is not to be seen as something inherent in their improved capacity for faith or their more intense prayer life, but is a result of their being endued with Jesus' own authority (see 9:16; 10:19). This will be important in the early church. However, Jesus then emphasises that there is something even more significant—namely that their names are written in heaven. In other words, they have 'entered the kingdom of God'.

If we rejoice at our capacity to achieve things for the kingdom of God, it is easy to start being proud of our achievements, even in the spiritual realm; then effective ministry can soon go badly wrong. To rejoice in (or 'boast' in—that is, place our confidence in) our total dependence on God is a safer spiritual attitude.

4 Rejoice, rejoice!

Luke 10:21–24

Jesus had his own reasons for 'rejoicing'. He rejoiced that God had 'hidden these things from the wise and intelligent' and had 'revealed them to infants'. Let's assume that this is a coded message; how are we to decode it?

'Hidden things' often means the things taking place in the heavenly realms—the things that require an 'unveiling' or 'apocalypse'. Here, presumably, what is happening is the coming of the kingdom of God, after Satan's fall from heaven (10:18). So who are the 'infants'? It makes best sense if we regard these as the disciples, those who have been involved in the recent mission of preparing the way for Jesus. They have experienced the powerful effect of the name of Jesus (10:17), and are those to whom Jesus has chosen to reveal his identity as the bringer of God's kingdom. To have 'hidden things' revealed to us, then, we need not merely an intellectual understanding but an experiential one. Those who obediently fulfil the mission of Jesus discover who he truly is.

Who are the 'wise and intelligent', who do not see? In view of verse 24, where we are told that 'prophets and kings' have longed to see and hear what has been revealed to the disciples, it is tempting to identify the wise and intelligent as them, but this is probably not right. These prophets and kings had the right desire; it was not spiritual blindness but their position in time that prevented them from seeing. So we are probably right to identify the wise and intelligent as the scribes and Pharisees, those who did not see because they did not want to see.

Perhaps it is even more significant for us to note that 'Jesus rejoiced in the Holy Spirit'. This is one of the few clues we are given that Jesus experienced 'charismatic'-like engagement with God. Taken with the content of verses 21–22, it also suggests (but does not, of course, prove) that much of the content of John's Gospel (see, for example, John 17) came out of the kind of dynamic, intimate spiritual experience that Jesus had, as indicated here by Luke.

5 The lawyer's test

Luke 10:25–37

'Just then'! How telling those words are. Jesus has just reminded the disciples that many from the past longed to see and hear what is being revealed to them. Now here is the living proof that people can see and hear and still not understand (see also 8:9–10). The lawyer wants to test Jesus, not see him truly, but it is soon the lawyer who is undergoing the test as Jesus seeks to open his spiritual eyes, his mind—first by asking him what the law had to say about 'eternal life' and then, when the lawyer wants to 'justify himself' (v. 29), by telling the parable of the good Samaritan.

The familiar title predisposes us to read this parable from the perspective of the one who is providing the help. It indicates to us that the Samaritan is acting as the 'good neighbour' character, even though he is despised by the Jews as heretical and outside the sphere of 'eternal life'. (Interestingly, of course, the Samaritan could have affirmed the lawyer's response in verse 27, as it comes from the Pentateuch, which were the scriptures that the Samaritans accepted.) Reading it this way, the parable affirms that we should be good neighbours to any who are in need, even our enemies.

This reading works for us in the West, as we are normally the ones who are standing in the superior position and giving out aid. For those who read it from the rubbish tips of the Philippines or the vulnerable position of some African states, however, a different reading is more natural. They read it from the perspective of the ambushed, wounded traveller, which indicates that those who are in dire need can accept help from anyone, even a Samaritan—or a capitalist or communist.

Reading the parable in this way, alternative understandings become possible. We might place the lawyer in the vulnerable position, as one who, if he were prepared to do so, might accept help from Jesus as his (eternal) life was under threat. Attractive as this reading is, however, Jesus' command to the lawyer to go and show mercy to all who are in need (v. 37) makes it problematic.

6 'Martha, Martha'

Luke 10:38–42

To gain a good perspective on this story, we do well to note the opening words: 'a woman named Martha welcomed him into her home'. These words imply so much about the family situation which we might easily overlook but which could be critical for a clear understanding of the story.

First, Jesus was Martha's guest and so she could have anticipated his gratitude. Second, the phrase also clearly indicates that Martha was in charge. Why this is so, we can only speculate. Was it because Martha was the dominant character in the family—perhaps the older of the two sisters—or because she owned the house? Was Mary there by Martha's invitation, especially for this occasion, so that she too could meet Jesus? We cannot be sure, and these possibilities are not mutually exclusive. Whether or not it is correct to link these two women with the Lazarus (and Mary and Martha) in John 11, it is notable that John also presents his Martha in a dominant role (see John 11:5, 19–27).

Whereas Simon the Pharisee is described (in Luke 7:36) as 'inviting' Jesus into his home (not 'welcoming him', presumably because he didn't offer Jesus the proper 'welcome', including foot-washing), Martha 'welcomed' Jesus (v. 38). We don't know who did the foot-washing on this occasion, but we do know that Mary sat at his feet (v. 39).

Martha had many tasks—presumably, all that was involved in getting the meal ready, which could have taken several hours. While she busied herself with all the organisation and endeavour, Mary remained in the position of intimacy and attentiveness, and, by so doing, perhaps she undermined Martha's intention of getting Jesus' attention and approval for herself. Could this point us towards the correct interpretation of Jesus' meaning when he spoke of 'the better part' (v. 42), a phrase that remains a matter of dispute? Is the heart of it that, rather than wanting Jesus for herself, Mary made herself available to him. Rather than wanting Jesus to look at her and be impressed, Mary wanted to discover all she could about Jesus because she was impressed by him? She recognised that he was the source of her life—unlike Martha, who saw herself as providing life-support for Jesus. Discipleship is about attending to Jesus, not doing things to impress him.

Guidelines

This week's reading provides many insights and challenges about 'discipleship'—following Jesus as Lord.

- Review the three cases of misunderstanding about discipleship (9:46–56). How are these human responses still manifested today? Consider whether any of them present dangers for your own discipleship.
- Review the three cases of people considering discipleship (9:57–62). How might we encounter such people today, and how can we help them to move forward?
- What signs of God's kingdom have you seen, either in your own church or at Christian conferences, or when involved in mission for Jesus?
- The lawyer had a real issue ('eternal life') but was 'testing Jesus'; Martha offered him real hospitality but appears to have been more concerned for herself than others, including even Jesus. How can we *nearly* get it right and yet miss the point?

1 The disciples' prayer

Luke 11:1–13

Discipleship is about attending to Jesus. What was true for Martha and Mary is also true for the unnamed disciple in verse 1. Presumably the disciples were often aware that Jesus was praying, but on this occasion a disciple took real note, asking, 'Lord, teach us to pray, as John taught his disciples.' The whole Christian church is grateful that he did so, as this prayer is one of the few things that unites all Christians. It is a special gift of Jesus to his church.

What is at the core of this prayer? Many books have been written, opening up its depths and riches. Such books often reflect the styles and preferences of their authors, and there is nothing surprising or wrong in that, for this prayer is comprehensive in its range and inviting to all shades of Christian spirituality. We can always discover more about its details, whether textual or exegetical. But the starkness of this short Lucan form presses home the question: what is at its core?

The answer is, I suggest, the relationship of Jesus with his God, into which he invites all of his followers. This relationship is expressed in the one word 'Father', indicating both intimacy and respect, both trust and obedience. It is more fully expressed and explored in John's Gospel (for example, chapter 17), yet here it is this word that acts as the 'entrance key' for all disciples. Paul expresses it by saying that the Holy Spirit enables us to cry 'Abba! Father!' (Romans 8:14–16; Galatians 4:6–7).

The whole prayer can be understood through the 'magnetic field' of this word and the relationship it expresses. The opening is all about the reality of God and the passionate longing for his identity to be recognised and fully restored on earth. It fosters the acknowledgement that God is the source of and provider for all aspects of human living, while imply-ing our dependence on him: 'Give us each day our daily bread.' The lines about forgiveness broaden this dependence while acknowledging the ten-sion between the reality of God and our own broken realities. Finally, the plea 'Do not bring us to the time of trial' not only reflects Jewish thought about the woes preceding the deliverance that God's Messiah would bring, but also highlights the vulnerability of all his followers.

2 The two kingdoms

Luke 11:14–26

Jesus taught his disciples to pray, 'Your kingdom come' (11:2), implying that the kingdom was not yet present (or at least not fully present) and, thus, that the disciples were living in an alien country, or at least under alien rule. For many who heard these words, their immediate thought would have been that Jesus was praying for the Romans to be defeated and overthrown. God's kingdom would oust the Romans, who were very much the aliens: this was assumed to be part of the role of the Messiah.

Today's passage makes it very clear, however, that this was not Jesus' meaning. Jesus affirmed that they were living under alien rule, but not that of the Romans—rather, that of Beelzebub or Satan. Among the evidence for Jesus' view is the suffering that Satan inflicts on human beings—in this case, a person who was speechless as a result of demonic oppression. Jesus saw all illness as an affront to God's purposes: this was demonstrated by his healing of the speechless man, as well as being indicated in his Nazareth sermon (Luke 4:16–27) and the mission of the Seventy (see 10:1–12, especially verse 9). In today's passage he adds a clear declaration of who the real enemy is.

Presumably those who accused Jesus of being in league with Beelzebub thought that Jesus must have been given authority by Satan over demons and was acting as Satan's general on earth: the demons did as he told them, even if he was telling them to clear off! By using rabbinic logic, Jesus establishes the flaws in the views of those who argue that he is working for Satan. Equally he shows that he himself must be the bringer of God's kingdom.

There is a twofold appeal to people to side with Jesus. First, he brings the challenge that if they do not join forces with him, they are actually on the side of the enemy, Satan. Second, he emphasises that seeking to maintain a liberal, open-minded, uncommitted position is not tenable (11:24–26). Although it is good to associate with Jesus and take an interest in his teaching (getting rid of the unclean spirit and cleaning the house), a casual association and interest lead to an unstable position. Only commitment to Jesus will prevent Satan from re-establishing his rule over our lives.

3 True blessing

Luke 11:27–36

In the previous passage, Jesus unobtrusively but firmly established his role as the bringer of God's kingdom: 'But if it is by the finger of God that I cast out the demons, then the kingdom of God has come to you' (11:20). Now he moves his claim a notch higher. Within his discourse are two astounding declarations—first, that he is greater than Solomon, the one who not only extended David's kingdom and was renowned throughout the known world for his wisdom but also built the temple, and, second, that he is more potent than Jonah. Through Jonah's (reluctant) preaching, the violent, corrupt, pagan city of Nineveh repented and was spared the wrath of God. (See the book of Nahum to get a flavour of Nineveh's reputation.)

Establishing his superiority over Solomon and Jonah is not the main point of Jesus' argument, however. His main aim is to challenge those who would associate with him too lightly—those who come hoping to see some miracle or other, or those who simply enjoy being in a crowd and listening to a good story (note the phrase, 'When the crowds were increasing...' in verse 29). His thrust is always to challenge people to hear and obey God's words, not to utter glib remarks (see vv. 27–28).

In Matthew 12:40, the reference to 'the sign of Jonah' is linked to the death and resurrection of Jesus, which parallel the time Jonah spent inside the great fish, but that is not the focus here. The focus is on the 'repentance' of the people of Nineveh in response to Jonah's announcement of coming judgement (v. 32). Jesus is pointing to the contrast between the humility and effort of the 'queen of the South', or the vigorous and committed response of the inhabitants of Nineveh, and the lethargy of his own hearers. What is needed is not glib, well-meaning praise, as from the woman who blessed his mother (v. 27), but true response to the word of God. Such a response was provided by the 'queen of the South' and the inhabitants of Nineveh. In this sense they are a 'sign' (vv. 29, 31)—a witness against Jesus' current hearers, who fail to see truly and respond accordingly.

4 Table talk

Luke 11:37–54

Martin Luther's 'Table Talk' (a collection of his sayings, taken from informal conversations) contains many strong comments. Here, Jesus at table is equally forthright, even though he is a guest, receiving hospitality offered by a Pharisee. Hospitality was a sacred requirement, but both host and guests were expected to treat each other with respect. This Pharisee was foolish enough to have critical thoughts about Jesus, noting that he did not wash his hands before eating. (This was a matter of holiness, not of hygiene.)

Jesus' failure to observe the holiness laws may have troubled the Pharisee because it had the potential to compromise him and his other guests. There was considerable anxiety about the 'contagion' of 'uncleanness' among the religious elite (see J.G. Crossley, *The New Testament and Jewish Law*, T&T Clark, pp. 51–66).

Jesus' first challenge, unlike the others in this passage, does not take the form of a 'woe'. It is presented simply as his response to the man's thoughts. This prompts the question of whether the following six 'woes' have been inserted by Luke into this dramatic context (compare the context in Matthew 23:13–36; Mark 12:37–40; Luke 20:45–47). Scholars can easily become absorbed in such questions, and, interesting as they are, they can divert us from the main issues (see v. 42).

At the heart of these challenges and warnings is the issue of the nature of our relationship with God, and, indeed, God's nature. In many instances, Jesus seems to align himself with the Old Testament prophetic tradition rather than the legal one, but he does so without quoting from the prophets. For instance, the directive to give 'those things that are within' (v. 41), rather than worrying about ritual cleanliness, echoes many passages, such as Isaiah 1:16–17 and Micah 6:6–8. However, these kinds of concerns are embedded within the more ritualistic commands and prohibitions too (see Leviticus 19, especially vv. 9–10, 33–37).

At the heart of Jesus' comments is the tendency he observes for self-aggrandisement and self-seeking within the religious leaders. The climax of his condemnations (vv. 47–51) relates to the hierarchy's persecution and silencing of the prophets (Amos and Jeremiah come to mind). Implicitly this puts Jesus in the company of the prophets and challenges the dark machinations in their hearts, which leads to Luke's summary statement about their antipathy to Jesus (vv. 53–54). There is a deepening sense of foreboding.

5 Coming out

Luke 12:1–12

In this passage some things are very clear and others are very ambivalent. First, Jesus is clearly warning his disciples of troubles that might be awaiting them. They might be killed (v. 4); they might be forced to speak against the Son of Man (v. 10); they might even be put on trial for blasphemy (v. 11), which carried the death penalty.

Equally, Jesus makes it clear that an open acknowledgement of who he is really matters. Verse 8 tells us this, but also a lot more. Acknowledgement 'before the angels in heaven' means that the disciples will be recognised as fit for resurrection when God acts to restore his new creation. 'Acknowledgement' in this context is not like having one's name considered worthy of inscription on a memorial stone. Rather, it is a public affirmation, in the divine law courts, that these people are authentic disciples.

We are also assured that we matter to God: we are of infinitely more value than a few sparrows. This parallel is significant. The disciples were not the peacocks of their world; they were the common people, without great finery, struggling for a living—like the sparrows. So this image would have had powerful resonance with them all, and so would the contrast: they were of far greater value than sparrows, even if they felt themselves to be at the level of common sparrows.

So much is clear; what of the ambivalences? What is the connection between verse 2 (about uncovering what is hidden) and confessing Jesus publicly? Or should we not be making any link between these ideas? What is the connection between Jesus and 'the Son of Man'? Jesus stops short of clearly identifying himself with this figure, perhaps to avoid appearing hubristic (he could not grasp such an honour, it had to be bestowed by God; see Philippians 2:6–9), or because it was politically too dangerous, or to prevent people projecting on to him the associations with 'the Son of Man' in popular thought.

What is the major difference between speaking against the Son of Man (whether this is Jesus or the redeemer figure of popular thought) and 'blaspheming against the Holy Spirit' (v. 10)? And why could the latter not be forgiven? The use of similar language in Acts 5:1–11 may indicate that this 'blasphemy' is the presumption that we can deceive God.

6 Rich towards God

Luke 12:13–34

Jesus said that we cannot serve both God and selfish greed—the god Mammon (see Matthew 6:24). Here, this point is explored further. First, Jesus the rabbi is approached to adjudicate in a family dispute over inheritance. Then, in amplification of his answer, we read another of Luke's memorable parables—about a rich farmer. Next we have some extended teaching to the disciples about trusting God for their daily needs, and finally comes the command and challenge to 'sell your possessions' (v. 33).

At the heart of all of this is the question of the depth of our trust in God and our awareness that we are privileged to be those whom God has chosen for his kingdom. As a lone farmer, striving against the elements, destructive wild animals, invading armies or even malicious fellow farmers, if your kingdom is your farm, then you will invest all your energy in increasing productivity and profit. But the death of the father whose son raised the issue of inheritance reminds us that our own kingdoms are limited by our lifespan. Even for whole nations that strive for resources and security (v. 30), the lessons of history tell us that their supremacy and success are time-limited.

The only true security, the only really wise investment of our time and energy and love, is God's kingdom. Jesus makes three closely related but distinct points about the appropriateness of trusting God. First, God is able to take care of us (as well as the birds and the flowers). Second, although he is Lord of the universe, he is not so absorbed with the big issues that he ignores our requirements: he knows our need for these physical things. Third, he is no mean master. He is our Father and it is his pleasure to 'give you the kingdom' (v. 32)—which includes providing for our physical needs.

Balancing these assurances are the challenges not to worry (to become absorbed and totally focused on our physical needs), and not to be afraid. We may find these 'commands' difficult enough, but, for peasant subsistence farmers or day-labourers living in an occupied country, what a devastating challenge they brought!

Yet the greater challenge is still to come: 'Sell your possessions, and give alms.' While the point might be a general one, the implication is that, by making this lifestyle choice, we are recognising the imminent arrival of God's kingdom.

Guidelines

'Lord, teach us to pray' (Luke 11:1). Do you think disciples should need help in praying, or should it come naturally to us? Who (or what) has helped you to pray? Do you need most help with what you should pray about—the content of your prayers—or with how to stay focused on God? Maybe you need to know how to order your life so that you make proper time for prayer, or how to prevent your prayer time from becoming a 'routine'. Are there clues in the prayer that Jesus gave us, or the teaching that follows it, to help us in all these aspects of 'learning to pray'? Who have you helped to pray—your children, perhaps, or Christian friends?

Jesus challenged the Pharisees over tithing 'herbs of all kinds' (Luke 11:42) but meanwhile neglecting justice and the love of God. Where might you be vulnerable to similar imbalances? Do you allow people's accents or lack of dress sense to put you off them? With worship songs, does the repetition of some words, or the lack of proper line scanning, distract you from the meaning? What else might divert you from the truly important issues in God's eyes?

'Whatever you have said in the dark will be heard in the light' (Luke 12:3). Reflect on your conversations this week. What have you said about other people, or in anger, that you would be embarrassed for everyone to know about? (Think not only of words spoken but also of emails, Tweets, Facebook posts and texts.)

1 Faithful living

Luke 12:35–48

As we read through this text of Luke, we seem to have reached a watershed. The focus moves towards the denouement as Jesus warns of the master's return. Over the next week of readings, we will see him bringing the judgement of division even within families, telling of the need to interpret the signs, summoning people to repent to avoid God's imminent judgement and, finally, lamenting the fate of Jerusalem (13:34–35). These chapters are like a spike on a graph—a sudden upward thrust of intensified activity.

If this is correct, then we can understand the two parables about 'watchful slaves' as indicating the kind of attitudes we should have, as those who 'strive for the kingdom' (12:31). Both parables are concerned with proper behaviour and attitudes towards the absent master—in the first, being alert (v. 37) and, in the second, working for the master and not usurping his prerogatives (beating the slaves and eating and drinking: 12:43–45). The second parable is probably aimed at those who are going to be leaders in the church: notice that it is Peter who puts the introductory question (v. 41). Those who are managing other slaves on the master's behalf have a heavier responsibility: they must not usurp the master's privileges because of the delay in his return.

In between these two stories is a short warning not to allow a thief to break in. Not only does this enrich the sense that we must stay alert; it also provides the interpretative key, at least as Luke understands these parables: 'You also must be ready, for the Son of Man is coming at an unexpected hour' (v. 40).

There is an endless debate about the exact significance of the title 'the Son of Man' and to what extent it indicates Jesus himself. In the light of Luke 9:58, we can identify Jesus with the Son of Man, but 9:44–45 suggests that the disciples were puzzled about exactly who Jesus meant. This saying shows Jesus linking the Son of Man with his death (see also 18:31–34). Here and in other later passages, such as 21:25–36, Luke seems to be thinking of a post-resurrection eschatological visitation. However, the 'unexpected hour' of judgement also takes place at the crucifixion, as John perceptively indicates (John 12:31–32).

2 The cost of the kingdom

Luke 12:49–59

In order to make good sense of this passage, it is helpful to start with verse 50: 'I have a baptism with which to be baptised.' Mark 10:35–40 uses very similar language in the context of James and John's request for the priority seats in Jesus' kingdom. However, Mark includes a parallel metaphor, placing 'baptism' side by side with the 'cup' that Jesus will 'drink'. We know from Mark 14:36 and the parallel in Luke 22:42 that the 'cup' refers to the whole experience of rejection and crucifixion. In Luke, the use of 'cup' in parallel to 'baptism' is missing, but we can take the crucifixion as the implied meaning here too, not least because, for Paul, the link between baptism and the death of Jesus was very strong, and Paul and Luke were companions.

So Jesus is saying that he knows a terrible fate awaits him and he lives with that pressure all the time. He has reached the stage in his ministry where he can't wait to get it over. But, as John the Baptist said of Jesus, 'He will baptise you with the Holy Spirit and fire' (Luke 3:16). Fire is a metaphor for the discriminating judgement that comes with Jesus (vv. 49, 51–53; compare 3:17). So Jesus' fate will have a devastating impact on those who reject him. Even households will be divided over him, in direct contrast to the prophecy in Malachi 4:5–6 that 'the prophet Elijah' would restore fractured family relationships. This is another part of the pain that Jesus carries: the unintended consequence of his redemptive ministry will be division and destruction.

Verses 54–59, then, are Jesus' appeal to everyone to understand the 'signs of the times' and to respond accordingly. This is the point of the story, or saying, about settling a dispute before it gets to court. People need to sort out their relationship and response to Jesus before the time of judgement arrives, when they will no longer be able to avoid the condemnatory process.

Jesus makes clear in these sayings that his approaching destiny will be costly, not only for him but for everyone associated with him. Now is the time to be ready for the coming of the Son of Man.

3 Responding to bad news

Luke 13:1–9

Death, whether by cruel intention or accident, seems to fascinate us. Take a look at the newspapers to remind yourself of this phenomenon. So 'some present' faced Jesus with the news of Pilate's violence against some Galileans. Although we have no independent historical evidence for this event, it is typical of Pilate's behaviour.

It would be interesting to know whether the speakers were fellow Galileans (Jesus was known to come from Galilee and, like Peter, might have had a giveaway accent: see 22:59) or people from Jerusalem. If the former, the information might have been brought out of grief and concern: they were hoping Jesus might have consoling words for them. If the latter, they might have been hoping to stir up Jesus' anger and get him to denounce Pilate, so that they in turn could denounce him. We will never know, but his response covers the deaths of these Galileans and the inhabitants of Jerusalem who were killed by the fall of the Siloam Tower. Jesus does not get drawn into their morbid tales, but uses both incidents to emphasise the urgency of the times in which they all live.

This incident, then, continues the theme of the previous chapter, as does the parable about a fig tree (vv. 6–9). Although the tree is only recently planted, the owner wants signs of a coming harvest—the pay-back on his investment. He thinks the tree deserves to be removed as it persists in unfruitfulness, but the gardener appeals to the owner for a final chance. Jesus saw his ministry as giving Israel a last chance. It was making the presence of God and his kingdom unavoidably real: that's what his healings and exorcisms were all about (11:14–23). Equally, his ministry made an appropriate response a pressing necessity. That response, as John the Baptist also demanded, would involve 'repentance' (v. 5; 3:3, 7–9) and fruits appropriate to repentance (v. 9; 3:10–14).

It is tempting, but probably erroneous, to see a connection between the 'three years' in verse 7 and the estimated length of Jesus' ministry. However, the emphasis on the urgency of decision and action is unavoidable.

4 Inappropriate behaviour

Luke 13:10–17

What does an 'unfruitful fig tree' look like in real life? The Pharisees were busy studying, discussing and arguing about the meaning of the law. They were busy working out new rules to cover the implications of the law to help people live properly. They were even busy keeping these rules themselves and checking that others did also. Isn't that being fruitful? No! Such people are like a fig tree with lots of leaves, apparently flourishing but producing no fruit (see Mark 11:13).

The deception indicated by such a tree is revealed here by the words and attitude of the leader of the synagogue (v. 14) with regard to the woman who had been crippled for 18 years (crippled by so much more than just her physical condition).

Although Luke identifies the speaker as 'the leader of the synagogue', he makes it clear that this man was not acting alone. In his response, Jesus speaks to more than one: 'You hypocrites! Does not each of you...'

(v. 15), and later Luke states that 'all his opponents were put to shame' (v. 17). So, although the synagogue leader might not have been a Pharisee, we are probably right to include Pharisees among the 'opponents'. Indeed, the presence of such opponents would have made the synagogue leader's challenge against Jesus more or less unavoidable. The leader would not want to be condemned by such 'opponents': they were dangerous.

The healing event and the challenging dialogue echo an earlier incident, in Luke 6:6–11. There, the scribes and Pharisees were looking for evidence to use against Jesus. Here, the 'indignant' official seems more concerned to protect the reputation of the synagogue than to applaud the amazing healing of the woman (v. 14). This contrasts markedly with the woman's own response to her healing. She is 'praising God', but her praise does not influence the synagogue leader at all—at least, not in a positive way. What could have been a higher purpose for his synagogue? It is noteworthy that, rather than addressing Jesus, he keeps on trying to generate antagonism towards him by muttering to the crowd (v. 14). Yet Jesus is the one who is producing fruit, by setting free from her bondage by Satan a 'daughter of Abraham'.

5 Act now

Luke 13:18–30

We normally read the two little parables about the mustard seed growing and the yeast energising all the dough as indications that the kingdom of God is quietly, secretly and rather slowly but inexorably accomplishing its task: the purification and ennobling effect of God's kingdom is at work in our world. With this interpretation, these parables are then sometimes contrasted with the more incisive ones, such as the hidden treasure, the priceless pearl (Matthew 13:44–46), or the return of the king (Luke 19:11–27).

However, the context in which they are placed here suggests that Luke understood them differently. For him, the emphasis is on the fact that the growth of the seed and the impact of the yeast have now been accomplished. The seed has now become a tree in which the birds (often understood as the Gentiles) are able to nest. The yeast has done its job and the whole loaf has been leavened. So the next stage is about to take place: the Gentiles will come into God's kingdom; the dough is ready to be put into the oven. A watershed has been reached.

This understanding, I suggest, fits better with the tone of the whole section. Jesus is heading for Jerusalem, where the denouement will take place. As he travels through the towns of Judea, he is constantly turning people's comments around to emphasise the significance of the times and the need for costly decisions about the place of God in their lives. So, in verses 23–24, the intellectual query about how many will be saved is used by Jesus to challenge people to 'enter through the narrow door' (compare 16:16: 'everyone tries to enter [the kingdom of God] by force') and to underline the shortness of the time left for a valid commitment. Loose association or a disinterested fascination with Jesus is not enough. The time for exploration and general interest is passing. Costly decisions are required now! Otherwise, the Judeans will find themselves excluded from the true people of God (Abraham, Isaac, Jacob and the prophets). Indeed, as implied by the birds nesting in the mustard tree, the Gentiles might replace them at the king's celebratory feast.

6 The grief of a broken heart

Luke 13:31–35

Sometimes Jesus sounds very harsh—for example, when he is speaking about woes on the scribes and Pharisees, or when he tells a parable like the one in 13:25–30. Was he gloating when he told ordinary Jews that they would forfeit their places in God's kingdom to Gentiles unless they made a decisive commitment to him? Sometimes, too, Jesus seems to be derogatory and antagonistic towards Jerusalem: in verse 34 he underlines the fact that Jerusalem has a history of killing God's prophets (see 20:9–19). How are we to read these kinds of sayings through the real heart-attitude of Jesus?

In some ways this incident follows the usual pattern. People come with news, a query or (in this case) a concerned warning. Then Jesus takes the expressed concern and refocuses on the real issue—the shortness of time for repenting and choosing God's kingdom and God's king! But here there is a profound difference.

'How often have I desired to gather your children together as a hen gathers her brood under her wings' (v. 34). Here we are allowed to glimpse beyond the rhetoric to the broken heart of God in Jesus. All his challenges to the Pharisees and all the parables he tells against the leaders are not irate vitriol; they are attempts to dislodge the stubborn, to challenge the prejudiced, to touch the hard-hearted, because Jesus includes them all within the remit of his call. They are all his 'brood', even when they act like a brood of vipers. In the light of Isaiah 6:9–13, Jesus is under no illusions. His longing and his appeals are necessary, as is the sowing of the word, but the outcome is fruitless: '… and you were not willing!'

So they will be left to their own devices. There will be one last appeal, when they will say, 'Blessed is the one who comes in the name of the Lord.' These words will be used by the crowd as Jesus enters Jerusalem (see Luke 19:38) and events move inexorably on to his death and resurrection. This act of the suffering servant might just open their eyes.

'We accounted him stricken, struck down by God, and afflicted. But he was wounded for our transgressions… and by his bruises we are healed' (Isaiah 53:4–5). Only time will tell—but, sadly, Luke knows what it will tell.

Guidelines

Re-read the Bible passages covered this week and ask yourself the following questions:

- 'What have I learnt about Jesus, his ministry and his mission?' Give thanks to the Father for all you have (re)discovered.
- 'How can I live like Jesus—who, knowing that death awaited him in Jerusalem, still told his disciples not to be worried?' (12:32–34). Ask Jesus to help you.
- 'What puzzles me about Jesus' behaviour and his words?' Ask the Holy Spirit to help you as you struggle to go deeper into the heart and mind of Jesus.

It is noticeable that 'miracles' are now far less frequent in Luke's account, yet Jesus claims that he continues to do them (13:32). Why do you think this is the case? Does Luke expect us to realise that Jesus continued his work as indicated in Luke 4:18 and, as it were, fill in the picture for ourselves? Or is it that miracles became a less significant feature of his ministry? Should we expect miracles today as part of the mission of the church (see 9:1–6; 10:1–17), or are they not appropriate at this stage in our mission?

There is much in this week's readings about the need to make decisive (and costly) choices while there is still the opportunity, as well as the need to live effectively in view of the imminent return of the master (the Son of Man). What can help us recapture this sense of immediacy in our churches? What differences might it bring about in individual and church life if we did?

FURTHER READING

E. Earle Ellis, *The Gospel of Luke* (New Century Bible Commentary), Eerdmans, 1974

I. Howard Marshall, *The Gospel of Luke* (New International Greek Testament Commentary), Paternoster, 1979

John Nolland, *Luke 9:21—18:34* (Word Bible Commentary), Word, 1993

Tom Wright, *Luke for Everyone*, SPCK, 2001

Transforming community

Living as followers of Jesus is meant to be a community activity. It was so for the group of followers whom Jesus called to be his apprentices. Many of them literally followed him from place to place, hearing his parables and teaching, and witnessing his power to restore wholeness and holiness. Just as you can't play a team sport on your own, so the Christian life requires us to be team players who train, learn and work together towards a common goal. Our goal is nothing less than transformation through the power of God's Holy Spirit at work in and through us—the transformation of ourselves, as we become more like Christ, and the transformation of God's world as we participate in Christ's mission to bring love, justice, reconciliation and peace.

Miroslav Volf, drawing on his own experience of running Christian education and formation projects in the USA, writes about how Christian practices shape behaviour and belief. He notes that Christian practices have an 'as Christ, so we' structure (Volf, p. 250). For example, as God has forgiven us in Christ, so we are to forgive others. Christ is our inspiration and our model, and our behaviour is to be shaped by regularly rehearsing and celebrating together the remarkable story of all that Jesus said and did, which is at the centre of the overarching biblical narrative of the Creator and his world. Our beliefs about Jesus therefore come to shape our practices, providing a model for us to imitate. Without such beliefs there would be no distinctive Christian practices. However, engaging in these practices together, gaining experience of welcoming strangers, forgiving, serving others and so on, often brings deeper insights into our beliefs, which in turn further inspire, motivate, guide and strengthen our practices.

The necessity of learning and practising Christian faith in community came home powerfully to me at a Messy Church conference in Australia in 2011, where Duncan Macleod of the Uniting Church spoke about 'Twelve Gospel Values' that churches need to live out. It was a 'lightbulb' moment for me in thinking how we should be making disciples in Messy Church—not through special courses but through practising being church together. I am very grateful to Duncan Macleod for allowing me to base these studies on his curriculum for community discipleship.

Bible quotations are taken from the New Revised Standard Version unless otherwise stated. Page references refer to books in the 'Further reading' list.

10–16 October

1 A welcomed and welcoming community

Luke 5:27–32

Jesus welcomed all sorts of people. This was one of the main reasons why Pharisees objected to him with scorn and contempt, saying, 'This fellow welcomes sinners and eats with them' (Luke 15:2). Jesus even recruited some of these unsuitable people to be his apprentices, including Levi the taxman. Later, at Levi's party, some Pharisees (perhaps peering in through the doorway or window) were appalled to see a rabbi sharing a meal with a mob of tax collectors.

The Pharisees were an informal movement for spiritual renewal. They were passionate about preserving the unique identity of the Jewish nation and faith. They aimed to keep God's law in every detail of daily life, and so they would never eat with the common people, whose standards of observance were less rigorous. To eat and drink with someone was to offer them your acceptance and friendship, so no Pharisee would ever dream of befriending tax collectors like Levi, who were blatantly collaborating with the nation's enemies, the Romans.

Pharisees avoid sinners; Jesus befriends them. 'Why do you do this?' the Pharisees ask his disciples (v. 30). Jesus himself answers them. As a doctor comes to the aid of the sick, Jesus has come to help sinners return to God (vv. 31–32). Jesus makes the first move, reaching out to save.

The way Jesus welcomed and ate with sinners was a controversial and powerful demonstration of God's grace, of undeserved favour and acceptance, and generous welcome and hospitality have been practised by Jesus' followers down the centuries as expressions of this grace. As the first churches began to grow, new Christians of very different backgrounds, status and race found themselves meeting and eating together—and remembering Jesus, their gracious, welcoming host, while sharing bread and wine. They were no longer strangers to each other but members of God's household (Acts 2:46; Ephesians 2:19). Church members and leaders were required to practise hospitality (Romans 12:13; 1 Timothy 3:2), to open their homes to Christian travellers, such as Paul and his mission teams, and to be ready (like Abraham and Sarah in Genesis 18:1–8) to welcome strangers who might turn out to be God's messengers (Hebrews 13:2). As Christ has welcomed us, so we are to be a welcoming community.

2 A forgiven and forgiving community

Matthew 18:15–35

A wise church leader once remarked, 'There's no such thing as a perfect church. If you ever find one, please don't join it, because you'll soon ruin it.' Jesus was under no illusion that his community of apprentices could live together in perfect peace, so he taught them how to be distinctive in the way they dealt with their disputes within the community, offering wrongdoers three chances to admit their fault and accept forgiveness (vv. 15–17).

Peter has grasped that Jesus' followers must become a forgiving community, but he wants to know exactly how much more forgiving than other people they should be (v. 21). To forgive someone three times was commonly considered a sign of a very forgiving nature, so Peter suggests a much more ambitious target. Will seven times perhaps be the perfect holy number for Jesus' followers to work towards? Jesus, as always, sets the bar much higher (v. 22). In effect there is to be no limit, because we will presumably lose count before we reach the point where we can stop forgiving a brother or sister in Christ.

The parable that follows describes a community where unexpected pity and extraordinary generosity are contrasted with appalling ingratitude and heartless violence. Notice how all the other servants in this community are deeply shocked by the man's failure to learn from and copy the king's behaviour (v. 31), so much so that they report him to the king, whose pity now turns to righteous indignation and condemnation (vv. 32–34).

Those who have been forgiven by the king must forgive like the king (v. 35), forgiving not only our brothers and sisters within the community of disciples but also other people beyond that circle, even our enemies (Matthew 5:43–45; 6:14–15). We must live out this principle of the kingdom of God or risk losing our place at court. This is the pattern for community life that we are to pray for and practise (Matthew 6:12; Luke 11:4; Ephesians 4:31–32).

3 A served and serving community

Mark 10:32–45

James and John are keen to be chief aides to Jesus when he becomes king (v. 37). This may be their mother's ambition too, because, in Matthew's version, she is the one who asks on their behalf (Matthew 20:20–21). Jesus' reply suggests that sharing his destiny will require great fortitude, but James and John think they are up to the challenge (vv. 38–39). Jesus then says that these places of 'honour' are not in his gift (v. 40). Of course, when Jesus reaches Jerusalem, he will not be enthroned as king; he will be crucified between two thieves, one at his right and one at his left (Mark 15:27).

The anger of the other ten disciples when they hear of the brothers' bid for special status prompts Jesus to call a halt to the journey and deal with the dispute. The behaviour of Gentile rulers is emphatically not the model that his followers should imitate. Jesus radically redefines leadership. Anyone seeking greatness must be ready to graft for others like a hired labourer, and those desiring the highest status must take the place of the lowest slave (vv. 42–44). Their model is Jesus himself, the master who has come to serve, who is on his way to Jerusalem to surrender his life so that others may live (v. 45).

Luke's Gospel places this argument about greatness during the last supper (Luke 22:24–27), making the stark contrast in attitude between Jesus' servant leadership and the selfish ambition of his followers even more evident. John, of course, describes Jesus literally taking on the slave's role at this final meal and washing his disciples' feet (John 13:3–10). The one they call 'Lord and teacher' performs this shocking act of humble service to help them understand the cleansing power of the death he will shortly die for them (John 13:7), but Jesus also makes clear that his demonstration of a slave's role is an example of love that everyone in his apprenticeship community must imitate (John 13:14–15, 34).

Paul, therefore, urges members of the church in Philippi to 'do nothing from selfish ambition', but to contemplate and imitate the servant attitude of Christ (Philippians 2:1–8). As Jesus humbled himself to serve us, so we are to learn to serve one another.

4 A led and leading community

Matthew 5:1–16

The verses about salt and light that follow the Beatitudes (vv. 13–16) illustrate the wider purpose of all the commands that are given in Jesus' Sermon on the Mount. The community that Jesus calls together is not only to be one of mutual love and service between the members; it is also to make a positive difference in the wider world.

Salt makes a difference: it adds flavour and preserves meat and fish. Jesus' followers, in the same way, bring out the full flavour of God's kingdom and stop the rot. Light, similarly, enables people to see their way and be led to safety. In John 8:12, Jesus declares, 'I am the light of the world', a sure guide for anyone stumbling in the darkness. Here in Matthew, though, he says to his disciples, 'You are the light of the world' (v. 14). His community, by living out the values of God's kingdom, shines with the light of Christ. People then see and acknowledge that God is at work, that his promised reign of blessing and peace is breaking in, as Jesus himself prophesied (Matthew 4:17).

In the Gospels, Jesus is often recognised as a prophet who is filled with the Spirit of God. He not only proclaims that God's kingdom has arrived but also demonstrates the reality of this arrival through his powerful acts of healing, casting out evil and raising the dead. He leads his sheep into the full life of the kingdom (John 10:2–4, 10) and teaches his followers to make God's kingdom their passion and priority, just as he did (Matthew 6:33).

Prophets in the Old Testament were people called by God to be his spokesmen. They were often also instructed to act the message out. Isaiah, for example, had to walk naked and barefoot for three years (Isaiah 20:3). Ezekiel laid siege to a model of Jerusalem (Ezekiel 4:1–3). Jeremiah bought a field in a war zone as a prophetic sign of hope (Jeremiah 32:9–15).

We are to be a prophetic community, leading the way, marching to a different drum, shining like stars (Philippians 2:14–15), carrying the light for others, witnessing to the hope and reality of God's reign and spreading the savour of the saviour by making a difference in the world (1 Peter 2:12).

5 A reconciled and reconciling community

2 Corinthians 5:14–21

Reconciliation means changing enmity into friendship. This is Paul's distinctive way of explaining what God has done for humanity: 'in Christ God was reconciling the world to himself' (v. 19). A broken relationship is restored.

Verses 18–20 say three times that God reconciles humanity to himself. The enmity is all on our side, the result of our wrongdoing. God does not need to change his attitude to us. 'God proves his love for us', Paul writes in Romans 5:6–10, in that while we were still sinners and enemies, he reconciled us to himself through the death of his Son.

Reconciliation in Christ transforms the way we relate to others as a 'new creation' and a new community (v. 17). God's plan 'to gather up all things' in Christ is under way (Ephesians 1:10), for Christ's death has demolished the dividing wall of hostility between Jew and Gentile and created 'one new humanity' united with the Father, through the Son in the Holy Spirit (Ephesians 2:11–22). This new community, God's household and temple, is a prophetic sign of his reign of peace.

Reconciliation was also a prominent theme of Jesus' ministry and message. He welcomed sinners and reinstated Zacchaeus as a 'son of Abraham' (Luke 19:9). Many 'outsiders'—people afflicted with disease, disabilities and evil spirits—were healed by Jesus and brought back into God's community. 'Blessed are the peacemakers', Jesus taught, because by making peace between people they reflect the character of their heavenly Father (Matthew 5:9). His followers were commanded to love their enemies and be reconciled to one another (Matthew 5:23–24, 43–45; 18:15). In Jesus' parable of the two sons in Luke 15:11–32, the father is eager to reconcile both sons to himself and each other, but the elder son shows none of his father's peacemaking character. We are left to wonder, did the elder son remain outside and estranged, or did his father persuade him to join the party?

Reconciled sons and daughters of God join the community to which the Father has entrusted Christ's reconciling ministry and message (vv. 18–19). We learn to live peaceably with all (Romans 12:18), removing walls of prejudice, fear and enmity.

6 A consoled and consoling community

2 Corinthians 1:3–11

The apostle Paul suffered much mental anguish, physical hardship and danger as a messenger of the crucified and risen Christ. He accepted suffering without complaint as a way for God to demonstrate through Paul's life the life-giving power of the gospel, 'always carrying in the body the death of Jesus, so that the life of Jesus may also be made visible in our bodies' (2 Corinthians 4:10). Paul praises 'the God of all consolation' (1:3), who comforts and encourages him so abundantly in the sufferings of Christ that he in turn can share consolation with the Corinthians in their sufferings (vv. 4–6).

The 'we' in these verses clearly means Paul and his mission team, but the experience Paul describes is a general principle of the Christian life that holds true for the whole community of the church as they share in Paul's sufferings as well as his comfort (v. 7). The fact that all Christians do indeed share in suffering and consolation is made explicit in Paul's teaching about the body of Christ in 1 Corinthians 12:26: if one part of your body is injured, your whole body suffers. The same is true of the members that make up the body of Christ. The church community suffers together and rejoices together. This community of compassion and consolation is not limited to the local church, but also embraces the whole network of churches in other regions and lands. This is why Paul's collection for the believers suffering from famine in Jerusalem was so important to him as an expression of the solidarity of the body of Christ in suffering and consolation (see 2 Corinthians 8—9).

It is as we have compassion, suffering with others and sharing God's overflowing comfort and hope with them, that the body of Christ becomes recognisably like Jesus, who revealed the compassionate heart of 'the Father of mercies' by weeping at the grave of Lazarus (John 11:35) and showing deep compassion for crowds of helpless and hungry people and sick and sorrowing individuals (see Matthew 9:36; 14:14; Mark 1:41; Luke 7:13).

Guidelines

The Gospels show that Jesus came as a prophet, proclaiming and demonstrating the coming of God's kingdom. He came as a priest to reconcile us to God and bring forgiveness and healing. He came as a king to welcome sinners to his banquet. He came as a servant to give his life as a ransom for many. The church as the body of Christ, a kingdom of priests empowered by the Spirit of prophecy and servanthood, must learn to live out all four of these facets of Jesus' life and mission.

As we saw in the introduction, beliefs shape practices, but practices often precede beliefs. People often start praying before they really believe in prayer. They may join in with worship initially because they enjoy singing and want to belong to the choir, and then gradually come to know the Lord they are worshipping. They may help out with a social project because they feel they ought to serve their community, and discover through serving alongside other Christians how Christ the servant gave his life for them. But these faith journeys depend on there being a community that practises what it believes and demonstrates the fullness of life in Christ.

Considering our own local communities of faith, what do we think are the strengths and weaknesses of our community discipleship? What particular aspects require of us more rehearsal and practice, more dependence on the grace of God and the enabling power of the Holy Spirit?

1 A healed and healing community

Mark 5:25–34

'I am the good doctor' is not a recorded saying of Jesus in the Gospels. Jesus did, however, use the analogy of a doctor visiting the sick to explain why he ate with sinners (Mark 2:17). Notice how Mark in this passage casts Jesus in the role of the good physician by providing extra medical details that do not appear in Matthew or Luke: the poor woman has spent all her money on unpleasant treatments from numerous physicians (v. 26). Her case seems hopeless, but simply having faith to touch Jesus the 'good doctor' brings immediate and complete healing. She has been made whole and restored to her community. She has been 'healed' and 'saved' (the Greek verb has both meanings).

Jesus' many healings were signs that the message he preached was true: God's promised kingdom of salvation, peace and blessing was breaking in with power to heal, restore and make people whole, as foretold by Isaiah the prophet (Isaiah 35:5–6). When John the Baptist, imprisoned by Herod, sent his followers to ask Jesus whether or not he was God's chosen one, the Messiah, Jesus answered by echoing Isaiah's prophecies, telling the messengers to report back to John the many healings that pointed to the arrival of God's kingdom along with his chosen king (Matthew 11:2–5).

Jesus authorised the Twelve and, later, 70 (or 72) of his disciples to preach the same message about the kingdom of God and to heal the sick (Luke 9:1; 10:1). After Pentecost, it was the apostles mainly who continued to heal in Jesus' name (see Acts 3:1–10; 5:12–16), but not exclusively: Ananias was sent to restore Paul's sight in Acts 9:17–18.

Paul, as an apostle, healed many sick people but he lists 'healings' among various gifts that the Holy Spirit gives to the body of Christ, implying that these gifts might be given to any member (1 Corinthians 12:9, 28–29). James implies the same by commending anointing and prayer for healing for one another in the local church (James 5:14–16). The church is a healed and healing community, a witness through prayer and practical care to the saving power of Jesus our great physician.

2 An empowered and empowering community

Acts 2:1–18

Jesus begins his ministry in Luke's Gospel by claiming to be the one anointed with the Spirit of the Lord and sent to fulfil the prophecy of Isaiah 61. His prophetic commission is to announce good news of the arrival of an era of blessing, liberation and empowerment of the weak (Luke 4:14–21). At the end of Luke and the beginning of Acts, there is a similar emphasis on the Spirit as Jesus commissions his apprentices to be sent out in the power of the same Spirit to participate in his ongoing prophetic ministry (Luke 24:49; Acts 1:2, 4–5, 8). Without the gift of the

Holy Spirit that anointed Jesus, the participation of this small band of weak and fearful disciples in his ongoing mission is impossible.

In the Old Testament, God gives the Holy Spirit to empower and enable particular individuals, like Moses, so that they can serve God's purposes and speak God's word. When Moses is given 70 assistants to help him with the heavy burden of leadership, they receive a portion of the same Spirit that rests on Moses. They all prophesy, but only on one occasion, and this is clearly an exceptional event (Numbers 11:16–17, 25–28). On the day of Pentecost, Moses' wish that all the Lord's people could be prophets (Numbers 11:29) is fulfilled. All the believers are empowered to be a prophetic community (Acts 2:14–17), to be Christ's witnesses, in their words and actions, to the ends of the earth.

Old Testament prophets were frequently persecuted for courageously defending the weak and speaking God's word against injustice and oppression. Jesus warned his apprentices that they would be hated and persecuted as their master had been (John 15:18–20). If we join Christ in his prophetic mission to bring good news of blessing and liberation to the poor, weak and oppressed, we can expect to share in Christ's sufferings. We are engaged in a spiritual battle; we need to encourage each other to be prayerful and equipped with God's full armour and the strength of his power, so that we can proclaim the gospel of peace (Ephesians 6:10–18).

3 A liberated and liberating community

Philemon 1–25

In this personal letter, Paul urges Philemon to receive back his runaway slave, Onesimus, who has come to believe in Christ through meeting Paul (v. 10). Philemon owned the house in Colossae where the church met, and Paul's argument is based on a theological vision of the church as a community of people from different walks of life who have become brothers and sisters to one another in the Lord's household (vv. 1–3).

So Paul begins with thanking God for Philemon's love for the saints (v. 5), and he prays that this experience of partnership and sharing (the Greek word is *koinonia*) will deepen Philemon's awareness of all the good that comes from their fellowship in Christ.

This prepares the ground for Paul's appeal (vv. 15–21). Onesimus the slave has become a brother in Christ to Paul. Philemon should therefore welcome Onesimus back in the same way he would welcome Paul, his 'partner' in faith. The word 'partner' is *koinonos*, from the same root as *koinonia*.

Paul's letter provides a case study on church relationships, our *koinonia*. Through Christ we have been freed from slavery to sin and adopted as children of God (Romans 6:17–18; Galatians 4:7). We are one in Christ, and have new relationships with one another as full siblings (Galatians 3:28). Imitating Christ, we love and serve one another (Galatians 5:13). We are the focus of hope for the final liberation of the whole creation into the glorious freedom of the children of God (Romans 8:19–22).

I happen to be writing this on the day the Church of England remembers William Wilberforce and other Christians who campaigned for the abolition of the slave trade. It took centuries for the church to recognise the sin of slavery and act upon the full implications of Paul's letter to Philemon. This is not surprising, given that Paul taught Christian slaves to remember that they were free in God's eyes but to remain loyal slaves as a witness to their masters (1 Corinthians 7:21–24; 1 Timothy 6:1–2). As brothers and sisters liberated through the death of Christ, we have to reflect afresh in every age on what being a liberating community means in a world where there are many forms of slavery.

4 A transformed and transforming community

Matthew 13:31–33

Many who heard Jesus prophesying the arrival of the kingdom of God were puzzled because they expected God's reign to come with immediate apocalyptic impact, with the judgement of evil and the establishment of peace. Jesus tells this pair of parables to illustrate that God's revolution begins small and apparently insignificant or invisible, but it inexorably grows and eventually has a wide impact.

The mustard plant was proverbial for growing vigorously from a tiny seed into a large bush, two to three metres tall, providing a nesting place for many birds. A small amount of yeast mixed into a huge amount of flour will, after a few hours, transform the whole batch into enough dough to feed over 100 people. Both these transformations take time, and for a while it may seem as if nothing is happening, but the outcome is inevitable and irreversible once the seed has been sown and the yeast has been added to the flour. God's kingdom has begun, is growing and will reach fulfilment.

Jesus makes the same point in the parable of the sower. He sows the word of the kingdom in the hearts of his listeners, and a harvest is assured (Matthew 13:3–9, 19–23). Those who get the message will become 'a people that produces the fruits of the kingdom', as Jesus declares in Matthew 21:43. We see this fulfilled in the early church in Acts. The small group of 120 believers grew to over 3000, and kingdom fruit was seen in their positive impact on the community through healings and generous daily support for widows and others in need (Acts 2:42–47; 5:12–16; 6:1–6). The movement developed, spreading out from Jerusalem into the Gentile world and gaining a reputation for 'turning the world upside down' with its controversial message that Jesus, not the Roman emperor, was the true king (Acts 17:6–7).

When the yeast of the kingdom is active in the church through the Holy Spirit, so that its members become an alternative community living out the values of God's future, then the church will make a difference in the wider world, developing oases of security and well-being that enable many to flourish.

5 A created and creating community

John 15:1–17

The vine, in the Old Testament, is frequently used as a symbol of God's people Israel (for example, in Psalm 80:8–9). A vinedresser's sole purpose in planting and tending vines is to produce grapes. A barren vine is of no use and even makes poor firewood (Ezekiel 15:1–5). God's vineyard was meant to bear fruit of justice and righteousness, but it produced only bitter wild grapes of injustice and evil (Isaiah 5:1–7).

In John 15, Jesus declares that he is the true vine, the fulfilment of all that Israel failed to be, and his followers are the branches (vv. 1–2). We will be fruitful if we remain in Christ, receiving his love and being pruned, reformed and shaped by his teaching (v. 3). Our purpose, says Jesus, is to 'bear much fruit and become [his] disciples', bringing glory to the Father (v. 8). Our mission is to 'go and bear fruit, fruit that will last' (v. 16)—to have an enduring impact as we serve the greater purposes of God.

The same point is made in Ephesians 2:10: 'For we are what he has made us, created in Christ Jesus for good works, which God prepared beforehand to be our way of life.' As Israel was chosen to be a light to the nations (Isaiah 42:6), so the church has been created in Christ to glorify God by sharing in his mission of re-creation, the reconciliation of all things in Christ (Ephesians 1:7–12).

Israel failed in its mission to bear good fruit for the healing of the nations. Our fruitfulness is assured only if we remain in Christ, the vine. This means learning to obey his commandments, in particular the command to love one another selflessly and sacrificially as he has loved us (vv. 5, 10, 12). The church community must learn to imitate and obey Christ. Then we will be seen as the salt of the earth—by, for example, leading the way in caring for the planet—and light for the world, by exemplifying God's new-creation values of hope, justice and righteousness. We will mix the yeast of the kingdom into all of life (Matthew 5:13–16; 13:33; 21:43).

6 A learning and wisdom-sharing community

Ephesians 3:1–11

The central theme of Ephesians is the 'mystery' of God's plan for his creation, the secret of life, the universe and everything. This secret, hidden for generations, God has now revealed to those adopted as his children through Christ, giving them 'wisdom and insight' into God's eternal plan to unite all of creation and all peoples in Christ (vv. 5–6; 1:8–10).

'Wisdom' translates the Greek word *sophia*, which was used to denote the highest wisdom about things human and divine. People in Jesus' home town were astonished to hear him speak with such wisdom (Matthew 13:54). 'Insight' is *phronesis* in Greek, which meant practical wisdom for living, like that of the wise man who built his house on the rock (Matthew 7:24).

God has blessed his people with divine wisdom concerning his will and plan for the whole of creation, but this wisdom is also practical, because it enables us to live wisely in God's world, in harmony with God's purposes.

Paul's prayer for the Colossian believers is that they 'may be filled with the knowledge of God's will in all spiritual wisdom and understanding', because this will enable them to lead lives that please God (Colossians 1:9–10). James similarly urges us to pray for wisdom 'from above', saying, 'Show by your good life that your works are done with gentleness born of wisdom' (James 3:13–18).

God has revealed his wisdom to the church, but it is also his plan to make his multifaceted wisdom known *through* the church (Ephesians 3:10). By living wisely and well, God's household, a united body of reconciled former enemies and sinners, is to be a prophetic sign to all creation, even to the greatest and most mysterious powers in the universe, of God's intention to unite all things in Christ.

God gives his wisdom and insight to the church, and we are to demonstrate and share this hopeful, peacemaking, reconciling, reuniting wisdom with all. Of course, from both a Jewish and a Gentile perspective, this wisdom seems foolishness, because at its heart is a man dying on a cross, as Paul says in 1 Corinthians 1:18–25. But God's wisdom is countercultural; it is wisdom for a world that God is turning right side up.

Guidelines

The essence of discipleship is a calling to become a learning community in fellowship with each other and with Jesus as our model and master, filled with his Holy Spirit, living his mission and making a difference in the world. It is hard to see how gathering to sit in rows and be led in worship and prayer from the front for an hour a week will provide all the learning opportunities and practice that we require in order to learn to live wisely and fruitfully, to heal, liberate, empower and renew.

How, then, should we reorganise our church life and reshape our weekly programmes so that we can learn together more effectively? We need to address this question if we hope to become more like this description of the church from John Howard Yoder: 'a church clearly visible to the world, in which people are faithful to their promises, love their enemies, tell the truth, honour the poor, suffer for righteousness and thereby testify to the amazing community creating power of God' (Walton, p. 148).

Community is not an optional extra for the gregarious, because it is through the diverse, reconciled and united community of the church that God has chosen to reveal his wisdom and his eternal plan regarding the new creation, the new heaven and earth, where the curse of Eden is gone and the leaves of the tree of life are for the healing of the nations (Revelation 22:1–3). Ephesians shows us that God's mission plan encompasses the whole story of creation, salvation and re-creation. This means that the church must engage with the world, not simply because Jesus commands us to love our neighbours and enemies, but because God has called us to join in his mission of love to the whole of his creation.

FURTHER READING

Duncan Macleod, '12 Gospel Values': www.postkiwi.com/2011/messy-ministry-context-in-sydney

Malcolm Brown (ed.), *Anglican Social Theology*, Church House Publishing, 2014

Paul Moore, *Making Disciples in Messy Church*, BRF, 2013

Miroslav Volf and Dorothy C. Bass (eds), *Practicing Theology*, Eerdmans, 2002

Roger Walton, *The Reflective Disciple*, Epworth, 2000

2 Peter

Even more than 1 Peter, this letter comes into the category of a 'general' letter, as it is not addressed to people in a specified location. Its authorship has been disputed: it is argued that the style and language are different from 1 Peter's, that this author depends on Jude, and that Paul's letters are referred to as a collection, indicating a date after Peter's death. However, differences in style and language could be due to the use of secretaries. Jude may be dependent on 2 Peter, or both may have made use of a separate source. There is nothing unusual or suspicious about the use of sources by New Testament writers. Furthermore, the reference to Paul's letters in 3:16 need not imply the full Pauline collection.

These notes assume the writer to be the apostle Peter, writing shortly before his martyrdom in the late 60s AD. Similarities between 1 and 2 Peter and the claims of the letter itself support this conclusion. (For a full discussion of the issues, see the books in the 'Further reading' list.)

2 Peter draws lessons from the past to guide believers in the present and to give assurances about the future. Chapter 1 concentrates on positive guidance for godly living. Chapter 2 focuses on warnings about the negative influence of false teachers. Chapter 3 combines both emphases, with particular reference to the future.

Important passages include the privileges and responsibilities of the Christian life (1:1–11), the significance of the transfiguration (1:16–18), the inspiration of scripture (1:21), the nature and danger of heresy (ch. 2), and the certainty of the second coming of Christ (3:3–10).

Quotations are taken from the New International Version except where indicated.

1 God's part and ours

2 Peter 1:1–11

Verse 3 tells us that God's divine power has given us 'everything we need' for life and godliness, whereas verse 5 tells us to make 'every effort'. It might seem as if these two things are contradictory. If God has given us everything we need, why do we need to make every effort? Peter doesn't see any such problem: note the phrase 'For this very reason' in verse 5.

Imagine a student who wants to research a fascinating subject but has limited resources. She goes to university and is introduced to the library. Suddenly she has everything she needs, but that in itself won't give her a degree. She needs to use those resources.

God has met every need in Jesus Christ: he has provided us with his own righteousness (v. 1), grace and peace (v. 2), his divine power, his own glory and goodness (v. 3), and his very great and precious promises. Through these, we have a way in to his own divine nature and a way out of the corruption in the world caused by evil desires (v. 4). Peter indicates the scale of these resources: a faith as precious as that of the apostles themselves, and grace and peace 'in abundance' through the knowledge of God and of Jesus our Lord (see John 17:3).

God has met every need but we must make every effort. Having a fully equipped gymnasium will not make you fit. You've got to use it. In verses 5–7, Peter outlines eight 'exercises' that add up to spiritual fitness: faith, goodness, knowledge, self-control, perseverance, godliness, mutual affection and love. The NIV uses the rather bland word 'add' (v. 5) in this cumulative list, whereas the original Greek hints at the extravagance of a rich patron of the arts who will spare no expense in putting on a production to outshine all his rivals. What we are aiming for is gold-standard Christian living.

Verses 10 and 11 have troubled some readers, who fear that our calling and election are somehow dependent on our own efforts, but the context assures us that they simply underline the two aspects of Christian living: God's part and ours. Note whose 'goodness' is indicated in verses 3 and 5. In verse 11, the phrase 'there will be richly provided for you' (ESV) uses the same verb as the one translated 'add' in verse 5, indicating again an extravagant excellence.

2 You must remember this

At the time of writing this letter, Peter did not have long to live. Though confident that his readers knew the truth and were firmly established in it, he was determined to keep reminding them. There are several lessons we can learn: time is short, however long we live; old age is not an obstacle to spiritual effectiveness; the legacy we leave behind is important; human memory is very fallible and we need reminding often.

At the heart of Peter's reminders are the centrality of Christ, the power and majesty that he displays, and the honour and glory that he deserves. Peter reminds us of three testimonies to Jesus associated with the transfiguration: the eyewitness testimony of the apostles (vv. 16, 18), the divine testimony of God the Father (v. 17) and the prophetic testimony of Old Testament scripture (vv. 19–21). (Compare Hebrews 2:3–4; 1:5–13 and 1:1.)

In verse 16, Peter refers to 'the coming of our Lord Jesus Christ in power' in the context of the transfiguration, supporting the view that the references in Matthew 16:28 and parallel passages also refer to the transfiguration, which prefigures the second coming.

In just three verses (19–21), Peter surveys the entire sweep of salvation history, as revealed by God. The word of God in Old Testament prophecy is certain—that is, 'completely reliable'. This assurance is expanded in verses 20 and 21: 'Prophets, though human, spoke from God as they were carried along by the Holy Spirit.'

Verse 19 takes us from the past to (for Peter and his readers) the present. In the coming of Jesus, those prophecies have been made (literally) '*more* certain', in that they were fulfilled in him. Note the present tense 'We have'. On the basis of those certainties, we look forward with confidence to the future. The word of the prophets, given by God and fulfilled in Jesus, points to events yet future (to Peter, his readers and us).

The word 'dark' (v. 19) has the sense of squalid and dismal, with associations of general neglect, but the dawn of a new day is coming when the light of a lamp will no longer be necessary (compare Revelation 22:5). On that day, the morning star (Christ) will rise 'in your hearts'—that is, not just as an objective event but as a personal experience.

3 It's not all good news

Chapter 2 begins with an ominous 'But…'. In contrast to the reliable truth revealed by God through prophets and apostles, there have been, and are, false prophets and teachers. How can we recognise heretical teaching and avoid its 'destructive' influence?

The first evidence is an inadequate view of the person and work of Jesus (v. 1): 'even denying the sovereign Lord who bought them'. Here in embryo are beliefs about the deity and humanity, the sovereignty and suffering of our Lord and Saviour. The second evidence is a lifestyle that is unworthy of Jesus (vv. 2–3). Christianity is not just a system of beliefs; it is a way of life. Verse 3 highlights greed as the false teachers' motive (see 1 Peter 5:2). Their 'fabricated stories' contrast with 1:16.

In verse 4, Peter turns from dangers in the present to lessons from the past, citing three incidents when God acted in judgement on wrongdoers. We are to be alert and aware of danger but it is not our responsibility to avenge (see Romans 12:19). Of the three examples, the first involves angels but the second two involve humans, where, side by side with the wicked who are punished, we find righteous people who are saved—Noah and Lot, 'a preacher of righteousness' and a 'righteous man'.

This may seem an unexpected description of Lot. We think of him more as a backslider, making selfish choices, moving nearer and nearer to the wicked cities until he moved right in and became part of them (Genesis 13:12; 14:12). We think of his weakness as he exposed his own daughters to moral danger (Genesis 19:8). Yet God chooses him as an illustration of righteousness. That's what justification is all about: not our becoming so good that God is impressed with us, but our being so bad that we can only throw ourselves on his mercy and accept his forgiveness and salvation.

Verse 9 is the key verse in this chapter, speaking about the rescue of the righteous and the ruin of the unrighteous. It directs our thoughts to the future: however unjust things appear now, it will not always be so. That is the lesson of the past and God's assurance for the future. All the way through, as Peter has been talking about false teachers, he has kept reminding us that they will have to face God's judgement (vv. 1, 3, 9).

4 More bad news

Knowledge of God leads to a life of righteousness and entrance into Christ's eternal kingdom (ch. 1). Conversely, false teaching leads to a corrupt life and God's sentence of condemnation (ch. 2). From verse 10 onward, Peter focuses exclusively on the unrighteous, using vivid language and imagery reminiscent of the letter of Jude.

The 'corrupt desire of the flesh' is manifested in rebelliousness, pride (arrogance matched only by ignorance), lust, greed and self-indulgence (for 'blots and blemishes', v. 13, contrast 1 Peter 1:19, where Christ is described as 'without blemish or defect'). The unrighteous never stop sinning or seducing.

Verses 15–16 compare their behaviour to 'the way of Balaam… who loved the wages of wickedness' (Numbers 22—24; Jude v. 11). Balaam was a prophet—unusually, a prophet outside Israel, but one who knew God. He fell into temptation through the love of money. These verses bring us back to the concept of 'the way', or rather the two ways—the straight way and the way of Balaam. In verse 16, two words describe his actions: 'wrongdoing' and 'madness'. In the Greek, it's a play on words—*paranomia* and *paraphronia*, meaning lawless and mindless.

The vivid language in verse 17 is similar but not identical to Jude 12–13. In a hot Middle Eastern country, such phenomena could be fatal (see Job 6:15–20). From verse 18, the emphasis is on not only the character of these men but also their influence. The problem is not just that they have gone astray but also that they lead others astray. Once again they are described as deceptive, boastful, lustful and depraved. Not content with their sinful lifestyle, they entice immature believers and lead them into ruin. Verse 19 reflects the teaching of Jesus in John 8:31–36. Verses 20–21 reinforce negatively the positive exhortation given in 1:10–11. The two proverbs in verse 22 feature unclean animals, the first being taken from Proverbs 26:11.

Throughout this section, we have been reminded of the future, bringing God's day of judgement, and the fact that evildoers will be punished (vv. 12–14, 17, 20–22). These verses contrast with the wonderful promises in 1:3–4 and underline the need for effort (1:5–8).

5 What is the world coming to?

2 Peter 3:1–10

In this chapter Peter once again underlines his purpose in writing (vv. 1, 8): remember; don't forget. Although his letter is not all good news, he writes out of a heart of love. 'Dear friends' (vv. 1, 8) is literally 'beloved', contrasting with the selfishness and exploitation of the false teachers. Wholesome thinking is shaped by words spoken in the past, which have lasting authority and relevance.

Peter outlines the entire span of world history—past, present and future—in summary form: 'the world of that time… the present heavens and earth… a new heaven and a new earth' (vv. 6–7, 13). These three phases are divided by two cataclysmic judgements: flood and fire.

The reference to 'the last days' encompasses the period from Christ's ascension to his return. Verses 3–4 describe the reaction of scoffers, those who mock. There is no logic in laughter. 'Following their own evil desires' indicates that it is not simply an intellectual problem but a moral problem: they don't want to change. Verse 17 will describe them as 'lawless'.

Verse 5 goes to the heart of the problem: 'they deliberately forget…'. Peter's account of the first phase of human history, following the outline of Genesis 1—9, starts with creation ('long ago by God's word…') and takes us to the flood. In the original Greek (contrary to the NIV), 'by God's word' occurs at the end of verse 5, and the phrase 'because of which' at the start of verse 6 probably includes both the water and the word. With a continuing emphasis on 'the same word' (v. 7), Peter reveals the future of 'the present heavens and earth': they are reserved and kept for fire, judgement and destruction of the ungodly.

Verses 8–10 answer the question posed in verse 4. Our concept of time is different from the Lord's. With two negatives and two positives (v. 9), the apparent delay in the Lord's intervention is explained. The day of the Lord, a theme familiar from Old Testament prophecy, will come 'like a thief', as Jesus predicted (Matthew 24:43). Judgement will be unexpected and inescapable.

6 Good looking

Throughout the letter, Peter has encouraged his readers to keep looking back, remembering the truth they have been taught. At the same time, they have reason to be looking forward (vv. 12–14). Beyond the fiery judgement, there is God's promise of a new heaven and a new earth, the home of righteousness (v. 13; Isaiah 65:17; 66:22; Revelation 21:1). This is something we can 'look forward to' in every sense of the phrase.

The question that opens verse 11 invites us to look inwards. Peter answers his own question: we 'ought to live holy and godly lives', for which we have God's enabling (1:3–4). Holy lives should be different, not in an obnoxious way but attractively different because of an inner purity. Holiness is not possible without godliness. God should be the source and sphere of our living. Prayer should be a constant experience, and faith should mark our every move.

Verse 14 adds three further qualities for which effort is required. We should make every effort to be found 'spotless', or morally pure. We should also make every effort to be found 'blameless'. This was the requirement for sacrificial animals, and our lives are to be a living sacrifice. These two qualities were the hallmark of the sacrifice of Christ (1 Peter 1:19), and the absence of these qualities was what marked the false teachers (2 Peter 2:13; see also Ephesians 5:26). Thirdly, we should make every effort to be 'at peace' with God. Peace is the umpire of the soul (Colossians 3:15). To this, verse 17 adds that we should be on guard against error—not carried away, swept along with the crowd.

Verses 15 and 16 add a very human touch (Romans 2:4 may have been in Peter's mind). It is not wrong to have difficulty with parts of scripture that are hard to understand, but we must be wary of using our difficulty as an excuse to distort them with uninformed conclusions.

The final verse contains a command: 'grow'. There are things that will hinder our growth, but Peter highlights the things that will enable us to grow. He reinforces the importance of knowledge (compare 1:2–3, 5–6, 8), although knowledge by itself is not enough. We also need grace, and both are available through our Lord and Saviour, Jesus Christ. Peter gives him his full title, leading into the doxology: we grow and give glory, both now and for ever.

Guidelines

- Review the letter and identify those areas of the Christian life that you would categorise as 'God's part' and those that are 'ours'.
- In what practical ways would you aim to 'make every effort' and 'possess these qualities in increasing measure'?
- Draw up a list of the features that made the false teachers and their teaching such a danger. What practical steps should you take to avoid the danger if you are (a) a teacher or (b) a learner?
- Peter's analysis of history (2:4–7; 3:5–7) is unlikely to be adopted in a modern educational textbook. How would you answer someone who rejects the Bible on such grounds?

FURTHER READING

Norman Hillyer, *1 and 2 Peter, Jude* (New International Biblical Commentary), Hendrickson, 1992 (mid-range).

Richard J. Bauckham, *Jude, 2 Peter* (Word Biblical Commentary), Word, 1983 (advanced).

Jude

For many people, Jude is best known for the beautiful doxology with which so many of our church services conclude. When we delve into the letter a little more deeply, though, we seem to enter a world very different from our own—a world of angels kept in eternal chains; Sodom and Gomorrah; the archangel Michael disputing with the devil about the body of Moses; Cain, Balaam and Enoch. What exactly is the 'garment stained by the flesh' and why should we hate it? We might be tempted to borrow a title from Thomas Hardy's novel: 'Jude the Obscure'.

Beyond this apparently impassible barrier there is a wealth of truth and wisdom waiting for us when we take the time and make the effort to discover it. The letter was written probably in the mid-60s AD or shortly after, to a specific but unidentified community.

Quotations are taken from the English Standard Version except where indicated.

1 Opening greetings

Jude 1–2

A characteristic of the writer's style is a preference for grouping things in threes (although he is not a slave to it—preachers take note). We see this immediately in his greeting, as he introduces himself by name (Jude) and in terms of his relationships, first to Jesus Christ (servant) and then to James (brother). Judah/Judas/Jude was an honoured and popular Jewish name, but it was brought into disrepute among Christians by the betrayer. 'Servant' (more literally 'slave') of Jesus the Messiah identifies Jude with the servants of Yahweh in the Old Testament.

James was the brother of Jesus (Mark 6:3), the leader of the church in Jerusalem and the author of the general epistle (James 1:1). For both brothers, however, worldly categories no longer defined their relationship to Jesus (see 2 Corinthians 5:16). The resurrection was the catalyst in this change (compare John 7:5 with Acts 1:14). Jude does not claim apostolic authority, which he sees as distinctive (v. 17). His introduction is a lesson in humility.

Following the letter writing conventions of the time, Jude next addresses the recipients. Although lacking any geographical reference, he has a specific group in mind, and again uses a triplet formula: 'called, loved and kept', embracing past, present and future. These categories can be traced through the rest of the letter and emphasise the initiative of God the Father and Jesus Christ, from whom, through whom and to whom are all things (Romans 11:36).

To be beloved 'in' God the Father is an unusual expression. Some later manuscripts altered 'beloved' to 'sanctified', along the lines of 1 Corinthians 1:2. The next part of the verse can be translated as 'kept by' or 'kept for' Jesus Christ. Being 'loved' and being 'kept' are key concepts throughout.

In verse 2, the greeting concludes with a prayer, once more in three-fold form. Mercy, peace and love—a unique combination in the New Testament—are ethical qualities. We must show mercy, be peacemakers and demonstrate love. However, New Testament ethics do not begin with our efforts but with God's enabling, which is available in abundance and appropriated in prayer. As in verse 1, it is God's initiative that is emphasised. In the teaching of Jesus, narrative, dialogue and illustration predominate over propositional theology. His parable in Matthew 18:21–35 illustrates this principle with particular reference to mercy.

Additional optional reading: Matthew 18:21–35.

2 Alarm bells ring

Jude 3–7

There are times when what we want to do is overtaken by what we have to do, and these experiences can be frustrating. Jude describes such an experience. What he was 'very eager' to do was to spend unhurried time writing about salvation—perhaps a lengthier exposition, similar to Paul's letter to the Romans—but circumstances put that on the back burner as a more pressing development demanded an immediate and urgent response.

Verses 3–4 illustrate two aspects of 'the faith'. Here it is not our personal response to the gospel but the objective body of truth on which our belief is based. It is something shared by all God's people and there is a completeness and finality to it (see Galatians 1:6–9). At the same time, there is a need to defend it against those who would add to or alter it, and it is the latter danger that so alarms Jude. He highlights the subtlety of the false teachers' approach, the serious consequences of their activity and the ungodly behaviour associated with their teaching. At the heart of the true faith is the grace of God and the centrality of Jesus Christ as Master and Lord, so false teaching perverts God's grace and deprecates Christ. Interpreting grace as a licence to sin is a misunderstanding of salvation (Romans 6:1–18). Denying Jesus Christ is the antithesis of Christianity, since the declaration 'Jesus is Lord' is the very essence of the creed (1 Corinthians 12:3; Philippians 2:9–11).

In verses 5–7, Jude uses three examples to illustrate the danger and its consequences. The Israelites whom Jesus (early manuscripts) or the Lord (most manuscripts) 'saved' in the exodus from Egypt, he later 'destroyed' because of unbelief. Angels who did not 'keep' their position of security and authority are 'kept' chained in gloomy darkness until the final judgement. Sodom and Gomorrah and nearby towns, which indulged in sexual immorality and perversion, exemplify the punishment of eternal fire. The first two examples warn that privilege does not guarantee immunity from sin and judgement. Rather, it emphasises the serious consequences of a fall from the holiness that befits 'the saints' (v. 3). For redeemed people and exalted angels to be bracketed with Sodom and Gomorrah is a truly shocking comparison. There is no place for unbelief, pride, rebellion, lust or immorality.

Additional optional reading: Romans 6:1–18.

3 Learning from history

Jude 8–10

From this point, the 'certain people' of verse 4 are referred to as 'these people' (vv. 8, 10, 12, 16, 19). The verb tense correspondingly switches between past and present as Jude shows how past prophecies and events illustrate the present danger created by the infiltrators, a danger that (he implies) these people themselves fully recognised. Knowing the danger is no guarantee of avoiding it. Where did they go wrong? Again Jude adopts a threefold analysis.

They defile the flesh, indulging in sexual excesses. They reject the only valid authority—that of Jesus Christ. They blaspheme or slander the 'glorious ones', a term used of angels who reflect the glory of God. Lust, rebellion and pride characterise their actions and attitudes, which they validate by their own dreams and visions rather than God's truth.

Verses 9–10 lead us into territory that is probably unfamiliar to most of us. Scripture records the death and burial of Moses in straightforward terms in Deuteronomy 34:5–6. The story Jude uses is from a Jewish apocryphal pseudepigraphical work, *The Assumption of Moses*, in a section that has now been lost. His readers' familiarity with it may have been a result of the heretical infiltrators' teaching, and Jude's use of it need not imply that he thought of it as inspired scripture.

Michael is the only archangel identified by name in scripture. While boldness might have been expected of him, given his authoritative position, he shows restraint in his rebuke to the devil, reminiscent of Zechariah 3:2. In contrast, the false teachers, whose only authority is self-sourced, have no hesitation in expressing their views in a way that is both blasphemous and presumptuous.

What lessons can we learn from this somewhat obscure text? To quote James 3:6, 'The tongue is a fire, a world of unrighteousness.' We need to watch our words—not to speak in ignorance, not to speak words that are destructive and judgemental and only demonstrate our conceit, not to respond as if moved by the instinct of wild animals. Rather, we need to use reason and restraint, above all honouring the Lord in everything.

The problem lies in both wrong attitudes and wrong actions. The false teachers displayed ignorance of God's truth along with a dependence on their own arguments and experiences, leading to immoral and corrupting conduct.

Additional optional reading: Zechariah 3:1–10.

4 'Woe to them!'

'Woe to them' is familiar from the Old Testament as a prophetic pronouncement of doom, but woe can also be an expression of grief, as in Matthew 24:19. In verse 11, Jude cites three Old Testament figures and associates the false teachers with them more closely by moving away from the present tense. Cain's pride led to godlessness, murder and ultimately banishment (Genesis 4:2–16). Balaam was hired to curse the people God had blessed, and later led the people into idolatry and immorality (Numbers 22—24; 31:16). Korah led a rebellion against the leadership of Moses and Aaron and perished in a dramatic judgement, along with other rebels (Numbers 16:1–35). Together they illustrate the results of pride, greed and jealousy.

Returning to the present tense in verses 12–13, Jude piles up powerful images taken mainly from the four regions of the natural world: air, earth, sea and sky. The false teachers are as dangerous as hidden reefs beneath the surface of the sea; as selfish as greedy shepherds; as misleading as clouds that bring no rain; as fruitless as trees that, having not fruited in late autumn, have been uprooted; as polluted as wild waves of the sea and as deceptive as 'wanderers'—here probably referring to planets or shooting stars, in contrast to fixed stars by which a safe course can be plotted.

In verses 14–15, Jude quotes from the book of Enoch, a popular writing of the day. The 'seventh from Adam' is an inclusive reckoning, as was customary (Genesis 5:3–24; 1 Chronicles 1:1–3). The quotation is particularly powerful with its repetition of 'all' and 'ungodly'. Jude applies the coming of 'the Lord' to the return of Christ. What is done, the way it is done and what is said will all be judged.

Such ungodliness is elaborated in five ways in verse 16. 'Grumbling' is a recurring fault in scripture, from Israel's wanderings in the desert to Paul's warning in Philippians 2:14. 'Malcontents' describes those who are always finding fault with others and with God. Their guiding lights are their own 'selfish desires'. Their arrogance comes out in 'boastful' words and they show 'favouritism' to those who can repay them in some way— the reverse of 1 Corinthians 13:4–7.

Additional optional reading: 1 Corinthians 13.

5 'But you, beloved'

In verse 17, as Jude draws his letter to a close, he shifts the focus from 'these people' and addresses his readers in a very direct way—'But you, beloved', repeated in verse 20. This picks up both the context of love and the urgency of the appeal in the opening three verses. Linked with this direct appeal are two imperatives, 'remember' (v. 17) and 'keep yourselves' (v. 21). The predictions of the apostles are quoted as authoritative. 'The last time' is the period between Jesus' resurrection and his return: all Christians are end-time Christians.

Three features of the false teachers have been predicted: they are scoffers (see 2 Peter 3:1–4), they follow their own desires, and they are characterised by ungodliness, revealing their attitude, their motivation and their conduct. Verse 19 links the predictions to their fulfilment, referring again to 'these people' and identifying three further characteristics: they cause division, they follow natural instincts and they do not have the Spirit. For the latter two traits, compare Paul's contrast between the natural and the spiritual in 1 Corinthians 2:12–16.

Verse 21 renews the theme of keeping and being kept. There is a balance between keeping ourselves and being kept by Christ, between loving God and being loved by God. Compare Paul's injunction to 'work out your own salvation' balanced with the assurance that 'it is God who works in you' (Philippians 2:12–13).

Once more there is a threefold amplification of the command, starting in verse 20: building yourselves up in your most holy faith (again blending subjective application and objective truth), praying in the Holy Spirit, and waiting for the mercy of our Lord Jesus Christ that leads to eternal life. Of note is the trinitarian emphasis in these verses and the importance of holiness.

Verses 22 and 23 remind us that those who have received mercy must show mercy. The danger posed by the infiltrators must not lead to an overreaction. Those who doubt must be shown mercy and yet the danger of false teaching must be recognised (it is as devastating and destructive as fire). The exact meaning of 'the garment stained by the flesh' is not clear but fear and hatred are strong concepts, and firefighters and fire-rescuers must ensure their own protection (compare Galatians 6:1).

Additional optional reading: 1 Corinthians 2:1–16.

6 God's light shines in the darkness

Jude 24–25

Reaching the last two verses of Jude is rather like enjoying a spectacular mountain-top vista after a particularly difficult climb. It is a doxology, an ascription of praise, a celebration of God's greatness, lifting our gaze from the gloom of utter darkness to the light of God's glory.

Just as God is able to keep the rebellious angels until the judgement on the great day (v. 6), he is able to keep (or protect) 'you' who keep yourselves in his love, and prevent you from stumbling—that is, from falling into sin or error. 1 John 2:10–11 and 4:7–21 remind us that the love of God involves loving our brothers and sisters, which will also guard us against stumbling.

The doxology moves to the future, when God will be able to present you blameless before the presence of his glory with great joy (compare Colossians 1:21–23). Three features of this future presentation of the believer are worth noting. 'Blameless' is a sacrificial term, used of unblemished animals suitable for offering on the altar. The presence of God's glory indicates unapproachable light and holiness of character. There is, therefore, a paradox in the third feature, the attendant great joy and exultation. How can guilty sinners approach such a holy God, 'jubilant and above reproach' (NEB)?

The answer is found in verse 25, where God, the only God, is described as our Saviour. (For an amplification of this word, see 2 Timothy 1:8–10.) His salvation is accomplished through Jesus Christ our Lord. It is only through the sacrificial work of Christ that we are saved and can look forward to being presented to God without fault and with great joy. The mediator is also the master: faith in Christ as Saviour involves submission to him as Lord.

Glory, majesty, dominion and authority describe God's character. Our attribution of these in praise to God does not effect any alteration in him but it puts us in our rightful place, acknowledging his greatness and submitting to his authority.

God is eternal. He exists before time, through time and for ever. For the past there is forgiveness, for the future there is hope, and for the present 'now' there is assurance. 'Amen' is the Hebrew affirmation, 'let it be so', giving us the opportunity to add our own personal response in worship.

Additional optional reading: 1 John 2:10–11 and 4:7–21.

Guidelines

- How do you picture Jude in your mind? Of the people you know, whom do you think he would be most like?
- What clues does this letter give to what Jude might have written, had he been able to keep his original plan of writing about 'our common salvation'?
- Draw up two lists contrasting the qualities of true believers and false teachers.
- In Acts 20:29, Paul warns the Ephesian elders, 'Fierce wolves will come in among you, not sparing the flock.' Jude's warning is against a more subtle attack, that of wolves in sheep's clothing. How might these dangers manifest themselves today and how can we guard against them?

FURTHER READING

Norman Hillyer, *1 and 2 Peter, Jude* (New International Biblical Commentary), Hendrickson, 1992 (mid-range).

Richard J Bauckham, *Jude, 2 Peter* (Word Biblical Commentary), Word, 1983 (advanced).

Exodus 25—34

When we turn the page from Exodus 24 to 25 we cross a chasm of several hundred years, in terms of the viewpoint from which the text is written. In chapter 24 we are in the wilderness with Moses on Sinai. In chapter 25, though still with Moses, we are constructing the tabernacle with a wholesale clarification of worship and liturgy. What we have here is a book with two major sources, one going back to the wilderness era, the other reflecting the period (c. sixth to fifth century BC) when the Jews were returning from Babylon and seeking to build a new framework of faith and worship—a new identity for a new community.

Exodus as we know it dates from the latter period; its writers/compilers were children of a post-exilic community emerging in an era of rapid social change. They seem to be trying to do two things—to link current developments with their history (Moses and those who came out of Egypt) in a constant and continuing relationship with Yahweh, and to respect and preserve those traditions in a new context with a view to restoring both faith and community. Chapters 25—34 may be seen as putting down markers—focal points of faith.

On a superficial reading it would be easy to dismiss much in these chapters as having little if anything to do with us, but God's word always has something to say. We need to remove a layer or two from the details and clarify the underlying significance, never forgetting that focal points of faith are just that—focal points, not the faith. Appreciating this ancient community's experience may be one step towards a greater understanding of our own.

The first week's readings are predominantly about the clarification and reconstruction of an institution. In the second week we move to more personal issues on the rights and responsibilities of the individual, making it easier to move from their world to ours. Chapters 25—34 give a fair reflection of the origins of Judaism, beginning with the escape from Egypt and life in the wilderness. Details suggest a later editing of the tradition and the addition of some new material, reflecting a much later time when Judah was picking itself up from disaster and seeking to rebuild both the temple, with new stones on the old site, and the community, with fresh expressions of traditional and long-established beliefs.

Quotations are taken from the New Revised Standard Version.

1 The ark of the covenant

Exodus 25:1–16

You don't have to be a detective to spot a discrepancy between the basic description of the ark of the covenant and the luxury surrounding it, nor to ask how runaway slaves in the wilderness could produce such expensive gifts, nor how the curtains could work in the open air and on the move. Here are two worlds, which helps to explain the confusing terminology (ark, tent of meeting, and tabernacle) subsequently.

Originally a simple box that contained the ten commandments (Deuteronomy 10:1), the ark's theological significance varied over the years. In the book of Numbers it is a sign of the divine presence on the battlefield; at Shiloh it is a symbol of the invisible God, and, in Jerusalem, God's 'throne'. This is a salutary reminder of how focal points may remain substantially the same but be differently interpreted, depending on time, place and circumstance.

Two things, however, remain constant. First, the ark is the focal point where God meets his people and where his people turn to meet him. Details of how that worked are in short supply and, not surprisingly, it would be different in post-exilic Judaism from how it was in the wilderness. Each generation has to find its own way of exploring that experience and the nature of its tangible expression, be it ark, tent of meeting, tabernacle, or whatever.

The second constant is that a continuation of the tradition still calls for personal sacrifice and commitment. Its very existence and maintenance depends on the willingness of the faithful to give it top priority, with sacrificial giving of their most valued possessions. Meeting with God does not come cheap, and the cost is not simply in monetary terms. Surrendering treasured possessions, traditions and convictions is painful, and reaching understanding and a common mind in any community can be a long haul.

Success depends on people recognising the focal point and contributing to it. Our gifts are crucial; the test is not what faith does for us—as if meeting with God were about collecting 'the goodies'—but what our gifts contribute to God's covenant of unconditional outgoing love, awaiting response. Such a focal point is treasured not for itself but solely as a means of meeting with God, and some benefit is derived from its mobility and flexibility.

2 The holy and the most holy

Exodus 26:31–37

What begins as a simple and uncomplicated concept—a box containing the commandments as 'a place for meeting with God'—doesn't stay that way for long. Most translations of 26:1 give us the word 'tabernacle' (Hebrew *mishkan*, 'dwelling place') rather than 'ark' (Hebrew *aron*, Latin *arca*, 'box or chest'). In earlier sources, meetings with God were more surprising, almost casual. Eden had no tabernacle; Adam met God unexpectedly in the garden (Genesis 3:8). So too did Jacob at Bethel (28:16) and Peniel (32:30), and Moses by a burning bush (Exodus 3:4), but over the years people seemed to feel either that an encounter with God called for something to identify his presence or that they wanted to know where he would be when they needed him.

New emphases and interpretations are not unusual with the passage of time, and, after the return from Babylon (after which 'the ark' no longer features), we have a generation seeking renewal. The change of word, with a consequential change in meaning, however, is not without significance. This tabernacle is not simply a place to meet God but the place where God lives; and the place where God lives must have 'curtains' and 'a framework', leading inevitably to a distinction between 'the holy' and 'the most holy' (v. 33).

Positively, this is a recognition of transcendence, along with the need for a place and a time. One wonders, though, if and when the tabernacle makers became aware of unintended consequences—such as the tendency to forget that God will never be confined to his dwelling-place and may well continue to appear to, meet and speak with them on many other occasions, as much of the rest of the Old Testament testifies. It is also possible that such unconfined encounters may be overlooked or dismissed as 'not quite the real thing', questionable or difficult to authenticate. Identifying degrees of holiness opens the door to a belief that some meetings with God are more genuine than others, or that some people (priests, for example) have privileged access, not to mention the hazard of encouraging the idea that a meeting with God can be arranged and possibly even 'stage-managed'.

Having a focal point is one thing. Having a focal point to the exclusion of all other points is something very different.

3 Conflict or compromise

Exodus 27:1–8

Picture a church (local or national) trying to pick itself up after years of turmoil, discussing focal points of worship—buildings, clergy, liturgy, ceremonials, and so on. It is committed, on the one hand, to beginning again and, on the other, to identifying the new with the old, partly to keep the traditionalists on board, partly to appeal to the revisers, and partly as a recognition that the community today is not what it was yesterday. Still in the wilderness this church may be, but it is a different wilderness, with people who have little or no recognition (never mind recollection) of what has gone before. This is the post-exilic community as it contemplates rebuilding the temple.

In the intervening years there have been many changes. In the wilderness, for example, the focal point for the community was the ark. By the tenth century BC it was a temple, often described as 'the tabernacle', with the term 'the tent of meeting' used to describe both. Different time, different culture, different structure, but fundamentally the same—a 'meeting place with God'. This whole chapter breathes a different air, but then some things must not change, as verse 8 emphasises.

Several questions arise. First, what do you choose to do (long term) and how do you go about it (short term)? Second, to what extent do you try to put everything back as it was, and by what criteria do you determine the new? Verse 8 suggests a victory for the traditionalists, but it raises another question: did the making of the altar really work out as expected or was that only ever a pious hope?

The incident focuses well the ever-present conflict for any church (or, indeed, any community) between dream (the past), reality (the present) and vision (the future). The dream was fine, the vision laudable, but the reality meant achieving the vision in a way that was practical and meaningful. Did it work? We have no means of knowing, but the rest of the chapter leaves us wondering whether the builders are fulfilling the dream or whether they are avoiding the issue by simply putting the past and the present side by side with a certain amount of incongruity.

4 Clerical dress

Exodus 28:1–5, 40–43

Aaron and his sons are still centre stage in terms of priesthood but there is an inevitable incongruity between then (in the wilderness) and now (reconstruction). Robes (clerical dress) are one factor. For us, what follows is more important for the questions it raises than for the detail provided.

First, what took the people down this road? One possibility is they wanted priests and temple rituals like those that many Middle Eastern temples had, and, if they were to pull rank with kings, they needed similar prestige and adornment. To what extent do we allow other faiths or cultural or secular factors to influence our choice of leaders and the way we relate to them? What do we expect of them, and with what consequences?

Second, underlying priesthood is an ancient understanding of holiness as contagious, closely allied to the concept of 'clean and unclean'. Yahweh is 'holy', and any human being or object that makes contact with Yahweh becomes holy, requiring special treatment. Paramount in this way of thinking is the Most Holy Place. Only the priest can enter it, and even he requires special clothing—which, by association, also becomes holy. How much this concept held sway in post-exilic Judaism is unclear, but these chapters certainly suggest that it was never far from the subconscious. Has anything like this filtered down to us, and, if so, where?

Third, do these verses have anything to say to us about clerical dress in today's world? The answer may be yes or no, according to your churchmanship, but two thoughts are worth pondering. Ephod and breastplate were very much the normal garb, different for priests only in the quality of the material and the costly adornments. Also, dress that is intended to honour the office nearly always ends up honouring the wearer. Though originally the appointed dress may have meaning relating to the job in hand (as some jobs require protective clothing), it is unlikely to be discontinued when the circumstances change; once the original intention is past its sell-by date, the tradition may even be fortified by other, more questionable arguments. But then, if we were starting from scratch, where would *we* begin?

5 Ordination

Exodus 29:1–9

Dress is but one issue calling for clarification and revision. With robes went authorisation. By the time the book of Exodus was taking shape, priesthood had something of a chequered history. Levites still enjoyed a special but not unique position within Judaism, and the boundaries defining the office were less clear. Evidence suggests that some were descendants of the old Canaanite priests, some had allied themselves to the monarch, and some were actually attached to the royal household. The latter relationship morphed into a natural allegiance, with a strong tendency toward imitation of the king (what was good for the monarch would be good for the priest), much to the chagrin of those prophets who maintained independence.

To appreciate what is going on, we must first put aside our understanding of ecclesiastical words such as 'ordain' and 'consecrate'. The variety of English translations unfortunately obfuscates the finer points of the Hebrew text, where 'consecrate' (Hebrew 'make holy') relates to 'clean and unclean', and 'ordain' (Hebrew literally 'fill the hands') relates to laying on of hands—a blessing or a gift. Then we must stand in their shoes and ask ourselves what they were trying to achieve—mainly, a link to the past (their origins), with an understanding of what had been gained and what lost over the years, and what needed immediate attention for their day.

For a people of faith, worship is the focal point. They need a place to meet with one another and with God. The ark encapsulated the idea but is inappropriate for their new situation. Surrounded by temples, they too need a temple. With the temple, they need leaders 'set apart from common association' (John Gray)—priests, or the like. Aaron is history, but they still need 'an Aaron' (perhaps more than one), identified and autho-rised, with powers clearly defined and limited, capable of maintaining the worship and the general direction of the faith. A priest will keep the faithful out of trouble (preventing them from becoming 'unclean') and will lead them into a wholesome and healthier way of life ('holiness').

Once defined, the priests need to be consecrated (made whole) and set apart (ordained), possibly with hands laid on, or with hands sufficiently filled, possibly with some symbol of office (the scriptures, maybe) to remind them of their privilege and responsibility.

6 Old, new or aberration?

Exodus 30:1–10, 22–33

Having established a fair basis for renewal, we suddenly find ourselves with fresh focal points on the scene, almost certainly from a later period and raising important questions. Are they genuinely new, refinements of the old, or 'borrowed' from another tradition? And why? Was it because of the failure or inadequacy of the established patterns, or simply weari-ness and a desire for something different? These are all questions we need to ask ourselves when confronted with new focal points of faith in our own experience. We need to look more closely.

The altar of incense is hardly new. On the surface it seems to be some-thing old that has been overlooked, but is it an 'old' thing that you would want to be associated with? It goes back to prehistoric times (third mil-lennium BC in Mesopotamia) and was not unknown among the Canaan-ites. Apart from a possible reference under Solomon around 1100BC, though, it was never part of the Israelite tradition; it was frowned upon by the prophets whenever it appeared, and was not even mentioned in Ezekiel years later. So was it a good new focal point or somebody's aber-ration? And why was it sufficiently important to those who compiled this text of Exodus to ensure that it was included?

Similarly, unction goes back to the second millennium BC, and is usually associated with consecration, healing and adornment. An early interpretation was that the aroma going up from the sacrifice enabled the deity to participate in the offering, but, with such detailed instructions for production, that could hardly be the case here. In pre-exilic times, it was usually associated with idolatry but here it is reserved 'for priests only', while the location of 'the tent' seems to put the emphasis more on separation than authorisation. So, once again, was 'separation' what they wanted? And if so, who wanted it, and why?

Focal points of faith play a significant role in all traditions, vary over the years, and are always subject to time and circumstance. In one sense, they are our creation; however, like our buildings, we may design and shape them but, once established, they shape us.

Guidelines

- Starting from scratch, see if you can design a new focal point, based on the ark of the covenant in Exodus, or identify other focal points that serve a similar purpose but are not necessarily regarded as 'a meeting place with God'.
- Beginning with your own 'meeting place', what 'treasured possessions, traditions and convictions' are you willing to surrender in order to maintain its essential purpose?
- Is our desire for a focal point about knowing where to find God when we need him or knowing how to avoid him when we don't?
- Reflect on a moment when you found yourself between a rock and a hard place. Did you choose conflict or compromise? Neither is a solution, so how do we handle this kind of situation?
- Spend some time thinking about the part that dress plays in our lives. 'Dressing up' or 'dressing down', and phrases such as 'men in grey suits' or 'women in provocative dress' carry strong psychological and emotive overtones. What does this say to us about the impact of clerical dress, and how might it help or hinder our thinking if we had to redesign clerical dress from scratch?
- What does the Hebrew understanding of 'consecrate' and 'ordain' contribute to your understanding of current practices?
- Think of some recent changes in patterns of worship in your own experience. What, or who, brought them about? Were they helpful and lasting, or ephemeral? What do you think was the motivation for the changes? Alternatively, reflect on long-established patterns and ask yourself how relevant and meaningful they still are.

1 The sabbath

Exodus 31:12–17

When we get to these verses on the sabbath we instantly feel on more familiar territory, and they give us plenty to think about. The Christian Sunday is not the sabbath, but the sabbath underlies the Sunday tradition and embraces elements much broader than simply 11.00–5.30 versus 24/7 shopping. It is also a good example of how a focal point of faith can show different facets and reflect different attitudes over a period of time.

Harper's Bible Dictionary describes the sabbath as 'a cornerstone of Israelite religious practice from earliest times' but what was it about? Some evidence suggests that its origins were more humanitarian than religious. Something similar can be found in Babylonia and possibly even in Canaan when the Israelites arrived, but, whatever its origins, the whole of the Old Testament sees it as a focal point going back to Moses and the wilderness experience.

The precise emphases are wide-ranging. Verse 13 sees it as a day to remember what God has done for Israel. Verse 17, casting a wider net, sees it as a commemoration of creation and a recognition of the link between God and his world. Two other principal features are that it is a day of rest and a day set apart for God, which is probably how most of us think of it—but that should not blind us to the other facets. The root of the word 'sabbath' is the same as the root of 'seventh' and most English translations of the earlier sources recognise this (Exodus 23:12; 34:21), in at least one case (Leviticus 25:4) relating it to a year rather than a day.

Radical change, however, came with post-exilic Judaism, when the earlier ideas were incorporated into the texts, with the addition of the humanitarian concept (Exodus 20:8–10; Deuteronomy 5:12–15) highlighting the day of rest. This then became paramount as a way for Israelites in a foreign land to mark their separation from the others. It was not exactly a new focal point but, maybe, a reworking of an old one with a fresh emphasis.

2 Forward to yesterday

Exodus 32:1–6, 15–20

This is one of those passages that all too easily evoke a self-righteous response. Those people had lost their faith, returned to the familiar, angered Moses and God and got their comeuppance, we think. It's always easier to revert to the old than to confront current problems, find a new way and move on. But self-righteousness can help nobody, and which of us can be sure that we might not have done the same?

Consider Moses. Was it a routine visit to the mountain or was this poor leader at his wits' end with the response he was getting from his followers. Perhaps he simply had to get out of the situation and chat with his creator. That might explain why, this time, he stayed longer than usual.

Next, look at Aaron. Was he a weaker character who could not cope with the mob, or was he part of the problem, not seeing eye to eye with Moses? Was he getting ready to seize his opportunity and take over?

Then, the people. Remember, they lost any focal points they had once had when they left Egypt. The ark was not filling the gap. With Moses present, either they could bear it or they knew they could not do anything about it. With Moses gone, the door was open for them to take the law into their own hands.

Now go back to Moses. Was he really angry, or consumed with disappointment to the point of despair? Either way, no wonder he threw the book at them and smashed the tablets. Fortunately, God is merciful. There is, no doubt, remorse on all sides, but God simply tells Moses to pull everything together and begin again.

Anyone who has lived through similar moments will see how frail we all are under extreme pressure—like a child who, when the whole world seems to be collapsing round his ears, needs to feel deep down that he is still wanted and have a place. Sometimes, in our worst moments, only God can give us that assurance. If reflecting on this story helps us to find it, we will be better people and the world around us may be better too.

3 The tent outside the camp

Exodus 33:7–11

These verses seem to belong to the early wilderness tradition and, on a quick reading, may be dismissed as having little of consequence for us, but when you scratch the surface two important issues raise their heads. Both are worth pursuing.

First, the Israelites' understanding of holiness was fundamentally tactile. Yahweh was holy. Anything connected with Yahweh therefore became holy by contact. This included people coming into contact with Yahweh, but also 'holy things', such as the ark, which contained the tablets of stone. To touch the ark, even accidentally, caused a 'contamination' that required purification, as Uzzah discovered when the ark was returned to Jerusalem (2 Samuel 6:6–7). Hence the need for the tent of meeting to be well outside the camp and have restricted entry. This is a dualistic philosophy: there is *God's* world, and there is *our* world (despite the fact that he created it), with few points of contact, and God's world is available only to a limited section of society.

With rare exceptions (in the way, perhaps, that some people view the reserved sacrament or the Bible), this is not what we understand by holiness. But then, what do we understand by holiness and on what foundation? Surely it suggests more than simply a person of integrity with a good reputation, which is what it has tended to become in popular usage. And where do we locate it—outside the community or at the heart of life?

Second, there is the issue of communication with the deity. Few will want to take verse 11 literally. Critics will ask how it could happen; cynics will wonder what language Yahweh used. But how do we hear God's voice? As an inner urge in a time of prayer? An unexpected nudge in a certain direction? A life of outstanding courage, or devotion in someone where you would least expect to find it? The thrill of nature or the joy of music? Writers such as Trevor Dennis, John Taylor and Gerd Theissen have a rare skill for hearing the voice of God (or sensing his presence) where many others would never notice it, and can inadvertently open our eyes and ears to similar experiences.

4 No-go territory

Exodus 33:12–23

The moment when God says 'No' or seems to thwart something that we have assumed all along was what he wanted is very much a focal point of faith. Can he be serious? Or are we misunderstanding him? Perhaps the experience of Moses can help us.

Here is a man with a great record of service to Yahweh. Despite all the problems and adversities, he has maintained his determination and his faithfulness. He knows that the incident with the golden calf was his nadir but he has repented, wants to continue and needs a massive vote of reassurance from Yahweh, which apparently he cannot get. The promised land is just over the hill and the people will enter it, but not under Moses (Deuteronomy 31:1–3). Yahweh will go himself (Exodus 33:14, REB) and with different leadership—an angel (33:2).

Moses must have been shattered. Having led his team successfully through every round of the competition, he is now to be denied a chance to play in the final. Surely not. He desperately needs reassurance and his plea takes two forms: for a special relationship with Yahweh, certainly, and to see God's face. Without this he cannot go on. Without it, how will his people have confidence in him any longer? But this is no-go territory (v. 20). Moses still has one more lesson to learn and Yahweh has his own way of teaching him. He is to stand on a rock; Yahweh will be there, but Moses will see only his back. Only afterwards can there be an assurance of Yahweh's presence.

This is the focal point where faith is tested. Not our hopes, dreams and ambitions that set us off on the quest. Not our plans and preparations; not even our commitment and determination, crucial though they are. All of that is by faith, not by sight. But then comes a moment when, out of the blue, we suddenly find ourselves saying, 'Yes, he was there all the time', and, on the strength of that recognition, we can continue in faith. Looking back at their history and looking forward to a new community, the compilers of Exodus knew exactly what that meant.

5 But what about the people?

Exodus 33:12–23

While Moses is undergoing this trauma, spare a thought for the people. What were they feeling? Leaving Sinai will be no less traumatic than leaving Egypt 40 years before. Forty years, in a wilderness, is a lifetime. Some can remember a time beforehand; for others, the wilderness is all they know.

Think of the changes in habits, customs and traditions over those years, not to mention personal relationships and friendships. How must all those trials and tribulations have affected their character? Some will have matured with the changes. Some will have gone under. Some will have settled for a kind of neutral detachment. Not one of these people is the same as they were when they set off. Some may have learned to love what they once hated, while others have developed an affection for the only life they have known. Promised lands, milk and honey sound great, but 'home' is where we have learned to live, and any new territory can be scary.

Then comes the news that the leadership is changing. Moses may not have been everybody's cup of tea, but at least they knew him. Life without him, in a totally new situation, was unthinkable. For many, Moses must have been a focal point of faith if ever there was one. To grasp the point, just suppose you suddenly discovered that your church life (local or national) was in for radical change, and were then told that the leaders who had brought you to this point, and in whom you have put so much trust, are not going into the new structure with you.

But the message is clear. Moses, sadly, cannot absolve himself from the responsibility for past mistakes and, in any case, is too tied into the old structure. He was fine for yesterday, maybe, but he is not the man for tomorrow. Like Churchill in 1945, he is the only one who could have successfully steered the country through war, but is hardly the man for peaceful reconstruction.

Finally, the good news. The future depends not on Moses but on God. He is still there and will go with them, although they may have to learn to relate to him in a different way. It's time for a new covenant.

6 A new covenant

Exodus 34:1–7, 10, 15–21

A new covenant—but are these new rules or a rehash of the old ones? The short answer is, a bit of both. Exodus has two versions (here and 20:1–17), and Deuteronomy 5:1–22 adds a third. Despite the biblical order, scholars regard the Deuteronomy version as the earliest source, the others dating from the later period of restoration and being woven into Exodus at the time of its compilation. That being the case, we have an interesting example of how a focal point may remain much the same for hundreds of years—still with mercy and forgiveness (*hesed*) and the faithfulness of Yahweh, despite the faithlessness of the people—but then submit to modification with fresh thinking and a new environment, leading to a variety of new interpretations. Fresh communities have fresh values.

At the risk of oversimplification, some scholars have suggested that we have two versions of the ten commandments, one ritual (34:17–24), the other ethical (20:3–17). Rather than compare them and see which we prefer, it might be more rewarding to ask two different questions.

First, standing in the Israelites' shoes, what does the difference of emphasis tell us about the community thinking that lay behind the commandments? All, of course, are attributed to the Almighty, but it is hard to think that there was no human input, if only in the way they were preserved, handed down, modified and still made central to the faith. Think of similar focal points in your tradition.

Second, who (then and now) would welcome these commandments and want to see them honoured, and who would not? Not everybody, for example, wants to live the life of isolation reflected in verses 15–17; clearly, many don't. Women seem to be overlooked altogether (v. 23) and shopkeepers were not overenthusiastic about sabbath regulations restricting work. So what sort of community is this and how has it changed over hundreds of years? Addressing, identifying and evaluating their focal points may tell us something about our own.

Guidelines

- Beginning with the link between God and his creation (ecology, resources and humanity), what does the sabbath have to say to us in a world that has gone overboard on 24/7? What have we lost and what do we need to restore?
- Imagine yourself in a situation of restoration, renewal or simply a rethink. The line is drawn between those who want to prioritise the ritual and others who go for the ethical. If you were a fly on the wall, where might you find yourself, and why?
- What do you regard as the predominant emphasis for today's equivalent of the sabbath? Are there ways in which we might bring our contemporary practices into line, particularly with the wider community in mind?
- Asked by a stranger where you find your faith, what is your first thought? The Bible or a novel? The church or the theatre? A Christian group or the workplace?
- Recall a couple of focal points with which you are most comfortable. How much do they relate to a world long since gone and how much to the world you live in today?

FURTHER READING

Bruce M. Metzger and Michael D. Coogan (eds), *The Oxford Companion to the Bible*, Oxford University Press, 1993.

John W. Rogerson and Judith M. Lieu (eds), *The Oxford Handbook of Biblical Studies*, Oxford University Press, 2006.

John Barton and John Muddiman (eds), *The Oxford Bible Commentary*, Oxford University Press, 2008.

Charles M. Laymon (ed.), *Interpreter's One-Volume Commentary on the Bible*, Abingdon Press, 1971.

2 Corinthians

2 Corinthians is one of the longest of Paul's letters but it tends to be over-shadowed by Romans and 1 Corinthians. This is a pity, since it provides a window into the life and ministry of Paul that is not available elsewhere, expressed in deeply personal and emotional tones in which Paul lays bare his heart and soul for the church.

As far as we can tell, 2 Corinthians was actually Paul's fourth letter to the church in that city. He had written an initial letter prior to the one we know as 1 Corinthians (mentioned in 1 Corinthians 5:9). Then, after writing 1 Corinthians, Paul's relationship with the church deteriorated. He visited Corinth—the 'painful visit' mentioned in 2 Corinthians 2:1, during which a particular individual caused him trouble (2:5; 7:12). Wanting to spare them another visit, he followed it up with a further letter (the 'tearful' letter mentioned in 2:3–4 and 7:8). As we read 2 Corinthians, we discover that this harsh letter caused the believers to deal with the offender and renew their support for Paul (2:5–11), news which was brought to Paul from Titus (7:5–16).

As Paul writes 2 Corinthians, probably from Macedonia (8:1; 9:2) in about AD55 or 56, he is planning a third visit to Corinth (12:14; 13:1). He prepares for that visit by first outlining his relationship with the church in the light of his apostolic ministry (chs 1—7), then encouraging them to follow through on their commitment to gather funds for the poor believers in Jerusalem (ch. 8) and, finally, defending himself against some who are calling his apostleship into question (chs 10—13).

Some scholars see chapters 1—9 and 10—13 as separate letters, because of the change in tone, but good arguments can be made for the unity of the letter, especially if it was written over a period of time during which Paul learned of new developments in the church and responded accordingly. It could be that Paul was holding off from tackling the more difficult issue until he had established his relationship with them in the early chapters. Paul commends his ministry to the Corinthians as one who has been appointed by God. For their part, an appropriate response from them will be seen if they complete the collection for the church in Jerusalem and reject the ministry of the false apostles.

Quotations are taken from the New International Version of the Bible.

21–27 November

1 Comfort in suffering

2 Corinthians 1:1–11

2 Corinthians begins, as many of Paul's letters do, with his name and a reference to himself as an 'apostle' (v. 1), a title that may well have been under dispute in Corinth. The fact that Timothy is added as a co-sender is not incidental (see also 1:19). With some exceptions, Paul uses the first person plural ('we', 'our') throughout chapters 1—9 as he writes about the nature of the ministry he has shared with his fellow missionaries.

The letter is addressed not only to 'the church of God in Corinth' but also to God's 'holy people throughout Achaia', suggesting that its contents carried wider implications than for just the immediate recipients. By extension, we too hear what Paul says, as those who have also received grace and peace from God (v. 2).

Paul includes a thanksgiving after his opening greeting (vv. 3–7). Unusually, he focuses not on some praiseworthy characteristic of the readers, but rather on 'the Father of compassion and the God of all comfort' (v. 3), who has comforted Paul in his troubles. In this way, his opening blessing turns into a moving reflection on consolation in suffering, which sets something of a tone for the rest of the letter.

Paul is clear that he received consolation from God in order to be a channel of it, not a container for it (v. 4). God comforts those in distress and then uses their experience to comfort others. All this comes about through Christ's own pattern of suffering, and for the benefit of others (vv. 5–6). The life of affliction and comfort involves partnership with the Corinthians, Paul says in verse 7, reinforcing his bond with them at this early stage of the letter.

Paul outlines a troubling experience that he and his companions have faced (vv. 8–10), but he doesn't say much about it. Most significant is the seriousness of the affliction ('we despaired of life itself'), God's deliverance of them, and the main lesson learned: 'that we might not rely on ourselves but on God, who raises the dead' (v. 9). This establishes a pattern that will become more evident as the letter goes on. Although Paul's hope rests on God's power to deliver, he trusts that the Corinthians will continue to pray for him (v. 11), and that this too will result in thanks to God.

2 Love in sorrow

2 Corinthians 1:12—2:13

Paul uses 'I' more than 'we' in this section, reflecting the personal nature of his relationship with the Corinthians, and he deals with some sensitive topics that could have damaged their relationship. At issue is the way he changed his plans to visit them and sent them a letter instead. Paul seems to be tackling an accusation that this showed his unreliability and lack of care for the believers. On the contrary, he explains, his actions were grounded in love.

Paul begins by defending his integrity in general (1:12–14), and goes on to justify the changes he made to his travel plans. What might appear to have been done out of self-interest was actually done because he wanted to spare the Corinthians a painful visit (2:1). He insists that he did not plan 'in a worldly manner' (1:17) and reminds them of God's reliability in keeping his promises (1:18–22). Just as God is faithful in fulfilling his promises in Jesus, so Paul may be trusted to act for the good of the Corinthians. So he admits that he did change his plans, and he did write a letter that caused them sorrow, but he did so out of love and concern for them (2:4).

In particular, Paul extends that love to someone in the church who has opposed him on an earlier occasion (2:5–11). This person is sometimes thought to be the man referred to in 1 Corinthians 5:1–13, but we don't know that for sure. In any case, Paul's 'distressful' letter achieved its purpose in persuading the church to exercise discipline, and Paul now urges them to forgive the offender, even as he has done.

Paul finishes this section by describing how an 'open door' meant he could have stayed in Troas to preach the gospel while waiting for news from Titus about the Corinthians, but he loved them so much that he couldn't bear to wait (2:12–13). The joy and relief that Paul experienced when he eventually met with Titus is described in 7:5–16. In between, he makes something that looks like a long digression, in 2:14—7:4, about the nature of the apostolic ministry. As it happens, though, this long passage is central to Paul's message to the Corinthians about the way of Christ.

3   Life and death

2 Corinthians 2:14—3:18

In 2:13, Paul leaves us waiting for the news that Titus was to bring about the church in Corinth—and it's not until 7:5–16 that he tells us what it was. It's as if he puts the issue of his relationship with the Corinthians on hold until he has outlined the nature of his ministry. For Paul, their relationship with him is best seen in the light of the larger story of God's reconciling work in Christ.

The images that Paul uses in 2:14–17 set the tone for the whole section. In view is a Roman procession in which the spoils of war, including captured men and women, are being publicly displayed as a sign of victory. The remarkable implication is that Paul and his fellow missionaries are like captives rather than victors. This underscores what will become a theme of these chapters—that God's power is shown in weakness, his glory in suffering. Like the fragrance from a sacrificial offering, the knowledge of Christ is spread through the apostles' ministry, which may lead to life or death, depending on how the message is received.

Although Paul claims to speak from sincere motives as one sent from God (2:17), he doesn't want his speech to be seen as boasting. The only letter of recommendation he values is the Corinthians themselves, who are inscribed on his heart and whose hearts have also been inscribed by God's Spirit (3:1–3). Paul makes reference to the law written on tablets of stone (Exodus 31:18; Deuteronomy 9:10–11) and the promises in the prophets that God would make a new covenant with the people by writing the law on their hearts (Jeremiah 31:33; Ezekiel 36:26). These promises give Paul confidence as a minister of the new covenant (3:4–6).

Paul is not denigrating the old covenant in 3:7–18, which 'came with glory' and 'was glorious'. However, in contrast to the glory that was veiled by Moses and was passing away (3:13; Exodus 34:29–35), the greater glory of the new covenant enables its ministers to proclaim it boldly (v. 12). New covenant believers who turn to the Lord have the veil over their hearts removed, in order to contemplate the Lord's glory and to be transformed into his likeness (v. 18).

4 Faith, not sight

2 Corinthians 4:1—5:10

The glorious ministry of the new covenant with which Paul and his colleagues have been entrusted means that they 'do not lose heart' (4:1, 16). They preach not about themselves but about 'Jesus Christ as Lord' and themselves as 'servants' (v. 5). Without any need to deceive or distort, they set forth the gospel plainly—which brings light, which in turn displays the glory of Christ, who is the image of God, and brings about the new creation work of God who shines light into the hearts of men and women.

And yet, Paul goes on to say in verse 7, 'We have this treasure in jars of clay to show that this all-surpassing power is from God and not from us.' Paul draws a striking contrast between the power of the gospel and the weakness of the container, which underlies the significance of suffering on behalf of Jesus, following the pattern of Jesus himself (vv. 10–11). Again, though, the pattern of Jesus' death and resurrection means that Paul can be confident that life will follow death (v. 14). Paul's trust in God who raises the dead enables him to keep going, knowing that it brings benefit to his hearers and thanksgiving to God (v. 15).

Paul's hope of participating in Christ's resurrection leads him to reflect further, in 4:16—5:10, on the differences between what is seen and unseen, temporary and permanent. In the present, Paul is 'wasting away' and experiences troubles, yet these sufferings are 'light and momentary' in comparison with the 'eternal glory' that God has in store.

Aware that the 'earthly tent' in which he lives could be destroyed, he reminds the Corinthians that 'we have a building from God, an eternal house in heaven' (5:1). Our temporary 'earthly tent', once destroyed, will be followed by a permanent 'heavenly dwelling', of which the Spirit is a guarantee (v. 5). Small wonder, then, that Paul says they 'live by faith, not by sight' (v. 7).

Although Paul clearly looks forward to a resurrected body, he offers few clues as to what he thinks any intermediate state might be like. Ultimately, though, what matters is not speculation about such things but a determination to please God, knowing that we are accountable to him (vv. 9–10).

5 One for all

2 Corinthians 5:11—6:2

Since 2:14, Paul has been describing the nature of his ministry, which is characterised by strength in weakness, glory in suffering, and life in death, as befits the pattern of Christ's own death and resurrection. As Paul brings this section to a climax, he deals with the nature of his message, which is about reconciliation, a significant theme elsewhere in his letters (see Romans 5:6–11; Ephesians 2:11–22; Colossians 1:19–23).

Paul begins by linking his ministry to what he has just said about future judgement (5:10; see 1 Corinthians 3:10–15). He is motivated by a healthy fear of the Lord, and what he is lies open before God and others (5:11); what matters, he says, is not the outward appearance but the heart. In addition, Paul is motivated by Christ's love (v. 14). Such love is seen supremely in the death and resurrection of Jesus, and it is those events of salvation that shape Paul and his ministry. What Jesus has done also affects Paul's outlook on others and on Christ himself (v. 16). Those who are 'in Christ' belong to God's 'new creation', which has been made possible now that God has reconciled the world to himself and committed to Paul and others the ministry of reconciliation (vv. 18–19).

2 Corinthians 5:14–21 provides one of the fullest explanations of Christ's death in Paul's letters. What allows God and humanity to be reconciled is that an exchange has taken place, whereby the sinless Christ became a sin offering for others so that they might become the righteousness of God (v. 21). It's on the basis of this that Paul can see himself as God's ambassador, appealing to people to be reconciled to God. A response is needed so that they too may experience the reconciliation for themselves and become part of God's new creation.

In the first place, this appeal is directed to unbelievers, but Paul also urges the Corinthians 'not to receive God's grace in vain' (6:1). To underline the significance of his appeal, Paul reminds them, using words from Isaiah 49:8, that the day of God's favour is 'now' (v. 2).

6 God and idols

As Paul brings this section on his ministry to a close, he makes some final appeals to the Corinthians (6:3–13 and 7:2–4), with a call to holy living in between (6:14—7:1).

Having just implored them not to receive God's grace in vain (6:1), Paul insists that the way he and his colleagues have conducted their ministry does not constitute a stumbling-block to them (v. 3). He commends himself only insofar as he is a servant of God for the sake of others, enduring difficulties and behaving with integrity, in spite of hardships. With his conduct in ministry backing up his words, Paul makes a final appeal to the Corinthians, reminding them that he has not withheld his affection but has opened his heart wide to them, an action which he hopes they will reciprocate (vv. 11–13).

Paul reinforces his appeal to them in 7:2—'Make room for us in your hearts' (picking up the language of 6:13)—reminding them that he has done nothing to prevent them from accepting him, and that he takes great pride in them (7:3–4).

In between the two appeals is 6:14—7:1, which appears to interrupt the flow. Paul combines rhetorical questions and Old Testament quotations to encourage the Corinthians to separate themselves from worldly relationships and to be dedicated to true worship of the living God. In the light of God's great promises, Paul encourages them to leave behind 'everything that contaminates' and focus on 'perfecting holiness out of reverence for God' (7:1).

The passage is popularly cited as a warning against marriages between believers and unbelievers. This may be an implication of Paul's words, but the wider significance for the Corinthians is probably to stress the need to reject anything that stands against the gospel, in order that they may be reconciled with Paul. Alternatively, it could be a warning against associating with Paul's opponents, especially those about whom he will write in chapters 10—13.

As it happens, then, this passage can be seen as part of Paul's plea for reconciliation—the climax of his call for the Corinthians to recommit themselves to him and to full restoration in the true worship of God.

Guidelines

In 2 Corinthians, Paul speaks personally and passionately about his own ministry, laying bare his heart and explaining some of the motivations and convictions that enable him to persevere in proclaiming 'Jesus Christ as Lord' (4:5). Paul is also clear about the sufferings that are likely to come the way of those in leadership (4:8–12; 6:4–10).

If you are a Christian leader, reflect on the ways your ministry has cost you, as did Paul's. How have you coped with this? Has God provided support for you? Give thanks for the people who helped you when you were struggling. If you are not in leadership, think of ways in which you can support your leaders and so share the burden with them, including praying for them.

Chapters 4 and 5 bring us some of Paul's profound insights about life beyond this life. Recall times when you have heard some of these verses used—for instance, at funeral services. What insights do you gain from these passages about our vulnerabilities and about our security in God?

1 Consolation and confidence

2 Corinthians 7:5–16

Paul began telling the Corinthians about his departure for Macedonia in 2:12–13, and he resumes from 7:5 onwards. In between, he has been explaining the nature of his ministry and the message of reconciliation that he proclaims. This may have looked like a digression from where he started in writing about his relationship with the Corinthians. As it happens, he has demonstrated that his relationship with them is a microcosm of his Christ-shaped ministry.

The seeming interruption of the account of his travel plans becomes, in fact, the heart of the letter—a portrait of authentic ministry. What Paul has written in these intervening chapters has to do with not just his apostolic ministry but also the tensions and sufferings involved in following Christ. All of this is in line with his experiences while waiting for Titus to arrive.

However, he was consoled when Titus arrived to tell him of the Corinthians' sorrow and concern for him (vv. 5–7). Paul's 'difficult' letter to them had succeeded, so he was happy, though sorry for the pain it had caused. It had led to repentance and eagerness on the part of the Corinthians to see justice done and to restore their relationship with Paul, which had been Paul's hope all along.

Paul writes further of his joy at meeting up with Titus and hearing how he has been refreshed by the Corinthians (7:13b). Before sending Titus to Corinth, Paul had boasted about him to the church there, and all that Paul had claimed about Titus was found by them to be true. In addition, Titus' own affection for the Corinthians has grown, and Paul feels able to conclude this part of the letter by saying to them, 'I am glad I can have complete confidence in you' (v. 16).

That confidence is significant in light of the following chapters, as Paul writes about the collection for poor believers in Jerusalem (chs 8—9) and faces down opposition to his ministry (chs 10—13). Titus figures prominently in the next two chapters (8:6, 16–24; 9:3–5), and this may be another reason why Paul has delayed his account of meeting him until he is ready to write to the Corinthians about the collection.

2 Grace in generosity

2 Corinthians 8—9

The account of Paul's relationship with the Corinthians, set in the wider context of his ministry of reconciliation, now gives way to an appeal to them to renew their commitment to the collection Paul is making for poor believers in Jerusalem. This was an important feature of Paul's ministry (see Acts 11:27–30; Romans 15:23–33; 1 Corinthians 16:1–4), possibly designed to allow Gentile believers to express their spiritual debt to Jewish believers, and to bring them together in a way that demonstrated the reconciliation made possible by the gospel.

The Corinthians had expressed support a year earlier (9:2) but had not followed through on their initial enthusiasm (8:6–7, 10–11; 9:3). Perhaps the rift between them and Paul had held up the gathering of funds. Paul now calls on them to fulfil their commitment.

Paul begins the section by describing the generosity of the Macedonian churches, who have given beyond their means (8:1–4; Philippians 4:15–16). Paul uses their example to encourage the Corinthians to resume their generosity (vv. 5–7). The supreme model, though, is Christ himself (v. 9, echoing Philippians 2:6–11). Their generosity is to be grounded in Jesus' own pattern.

A principle of 'fairness' comes out in 8:13–15, as Paul anticipates that the Corinthians' surplus will eliminate the deprivation of the Christians in Jerusalem. As in 1 Corinthians 16:2, Paul writes here about proportionate giving, calling for equal sacrifice, not equal giving. They are to give cheerfully and willingly, from the heart (see 9:6–7). Then, in 8:16—9:5, Paul outlines the steps he is taking to make sure his handling of the money is accountable and transparent. Along with Titus, he is sending others to be guarantors of the collection, to accompany it to Jerusalem.

Several key words recur throughout these chapters: 'fellowship' or 'partnership', 'service' or 'ministry', 'overflow' and 'eagerness'. Notably, 'grace' is central. The word is used to open and close the section (8:1; 9:15) and appears (though translated in different ways) a further eight times (8:4, 6, 7, 9, 16, 19; 9:8, 14). The motor for generosity is 'the gospel of Christ' (9:13), seen above all in the example of Jesus himself (8:9).

3   Edification and boasting

2 Corinthians 10

The expressions of joy and relief in chapters 1—9 give way, in chapters 10—13, to a tone that is more heated and direct. Paul's earlier use of the second person plural also drops as he makes a more personal appeal (v. 1).

The difference has led some commentators to suggest that these chapters were originally a separate letter, but they could just as easily be a response to additional news from Corinth received after Titus' report, which caused Paul to add material of a different sort. In fact, the change of tone could even be a deliberate strategy in the letter as a whole. As Paul prepares for his visit to them, he has outlined the nature of his apostolic ministry in the light of his relationship with the church (chs 1—7) and encouraged them to finish the collection (chs 8—9), which leaves him now to tackle specific opponents in the church head on (chs 10—13).

The identity of his opponents is debated, and we are left to decide on the basis of what Paul himself says about them. They were probably Jewish Christians (11:22–23), who claimed to be superior to Paul in rhetorical ability (10:10; 11:6) and disparaged him for refusing payment (11:7–11). Paul describes them as 'super-apostles' (11:5; 12:11), 'false apostles' and 'deceitful workers' (11:13), who preach a different Jesus, spirit and gospel (11:4).

As we might expect from earlier chapters, the essence of Paul's response is that the hallmark of an apostle is strength in weakness, following the pattern of Christ crucified.

He begins by responding to the accusation that he is weak when present but bold when absent (v. 1). To be sure, he doesn't fight as the world fights (v. 3), but he will use weapons that have 'divine power to demolish strongholds' and 'take captive every thought to make it obedient to Christ' (vv. 4–5). Having declared war on his opponents, he wants to make his intentions clear: he desires to build up the Corinthians, not tear them down (v. 8). To do so, he says, he is going to use the main weapon used by his opponents—boasting—but he will boast differently from them, rejecting self-commendation, and boasting in the Lord (vv. 17–18).

4 Foolishness and weakness

2 Corinthians 11

Paul makes clear to the Corinthians that he plans to guard their relationship with Christ against those who preach a different Jesus, a different spirit and a different gospel (vv. 2–4). He also defends his practice of supporting himself so that he can preach the gospel free of charge (vv. 7–11). He wants to show the church at Corinth what his rivals really are—'false apostles, deceitful workers, masquerading as apostles of Christ' and heading for judgement (vv. 13–15).

Throughout chapters 10—13, as in 2:14—7:4, Paul contrasts two competing patterns of existence. One sort of person lives 'by the standards of this world' (10:2), boasting in what is seen to be powerful and sophisticated, while the other discovers God's power most fully in weakness and suffering. In 1 Corinthians 1:18—2:5, similarly, Paul claims that God's power and wisdom are demonstrated in the cross, which looks weak and foolish to the world. It's in light of this principle that Paul concedes his opponents' basic point: he *is* weak, but it is precisely in such weakness that God's power works.

He illustrates his argument in 11:16–33, as he presents his own grounds for boasting. His 'fool's speech' (as it is sometimes called) is laced with irony, sarcasm and self-deprecation as he parodies his opponents' desire for praise and status. He acknowledges that he is acting out of character in making this speech, deliberately making a fool of himself, but he is adopting the convention of boasting about one's accomplishments in order to turn it on its head.

Paul provides a list of his trials—imprisonments, beatings, frequent and dangerous travel, general toil and hardship, along with his own sinful weakness and his anxiety for all the churches (vv. 23–29). His final example is particularly telling. One of the great honours for a warrior was to be the first to climb over an enemy's wall, demonstrating courage in battle. In a complete reversal of this picture, Paul writes about being lowered down a wall in order to escape an enemy (vv. 32–33)! The things he boasts about are all his frailties and failures. His real boast is in Jesus, whose power is displayed in weakness (v. 30).

5 Strength in weakness

2 Corinthians 12:1–13

It's possible that Paul's opponents have challenged his claim to be an apostle by saying that he has not experienced visions and revelations. If so, Paul sets them straight, but he does so once again by asserting one of the main themes of his letter—strength in weakness (vv. 9–10).

His introduction in verse 1, 'I must go on boasting', shows that the experience he is about to describe follows on from the previous catalogue of 'boasts'. The space devoted to it demonstrates its significance as the culmination of his argument.

Paul's use of the third person ('a man in Christ', v. 2) in describing the experience probably shows his hesitancy, even 14 years later, to sound as if he is boasting about special visions. He reports being caught up to the 'third heaven', or 'paradise' (although he is unsure whether it was in the body or in a vision), and hearing things that no one is allowed to tell

(v. 4). However, as we might expect by now, he directs attention away from the amazing experience to his weakness as the only safe ground of boasting (v. 5).

Indeed, to prevent him from becoming proud, he was given 'a thorn in my flesh, a messenger of Satan' (v. 7). The identity of the thorn has been long debated but remains unknown. Whether it was an illness, a physical defect, opponents, persecution, or something else, he asked three times for it to be taken away, but was told, 'My grace is sufficient for you, for my power is made perfect in weakness' (v. 9). So it is that, in verse 10, Paul gathers up all the troubles he has been describing since 11:23, summarising them as 'weaknesses... insults... hardships... persecutions... difficulties', saying that he delights in those things and declaring with respect to them all that 'when I am weak, then I am strong'.

As he did earlier (11:16–17, 21), Paul admits that he feels forced into foolish boasting (v. 11). He draws this part of the dispute to a close by telling the Corinthians straight that he is not inferior to the so-called 'super-apostles', and they should know this, given his demonstration among them of the marks of a true apostle (v. 12).

6 Building up, not tearing down

2 Corinthians 12:14—13:14

Talk of a third visit to Corinth dominates the closing paragraphs (12:14, 20; 13:1–2, 10), although Paul is concerned about what he will find when he gets there (12:20–21). For one final time, he returns to the cross as a model for his ministry among them (13:4). His apostleship and the character of his ministry take their cue from the pattern of Christ—of strength in weakness—resulting in a ministry that will build them up rather than tear them down (13:10).

Ahead of his visit, he reiterates his concern not to be a financial burden to them, as befits the relationship between parents and children (12:14–18). In fact, Paul makes it clear that everything he and his co-workers do, including his exposure of the false apostles, is to strengthen the church in its faith (v. 19).

A third visit could mean that Paul will discipline members of the church when he arrives (13:1–4), although he doesn't want to, and he asks them to examine themselves to make sure they are in the faith. Even here, Paul's love for the Corinthians shines through, as his main concern is not his reputation or their opinion of him but their spiritual welfare (v. 7). As he draws to a close, Paul sums up his reasons for taking the time to write this long letter: 'that when I come I may not have to be harsh in my use of authority—the authority the Lord gave me for building you up, not for tearing you down' (v. 10).

After his concluding encouragement and greetings comes the well-known 'grace' of 13:14, the only place where the Father, Son and Holy Spirit come together in a blessing. This is by no means a fully formed doctrine of the Trinity, but it's a clear indication that all three members of the Godhead were understood to be at work in the lives of the early Christians. The grace of Christ (see 8:9), the love of God and the fellowship created by the Holy Spirit can all be seen in the triune God's own work, and Paul now prays that they may be among the Corinthians themselves.

Guidelines

Paul's calling as an apostle follows the pattern of Jesus' death and resurrection (4:10; 13:4), yet all Christians are to embody the self-giving way of Jesus. It's the pattern of the cross and the resurrection that allows us to see weakness as a context in which God's grace can flourish, as Paul makes clear in every part of this letter. How has engaging with the letter helped you to accept your own weaknesses more deeply? Where can you see God's grace as 'sufficient' in your own life? Pray for those who are struggling with debilitating illnesses or circumstances.

There is much in chapters 8 and 9 about Christian giving. What insights did you gain and how might they affect the ways you give, both to Christian work and to other good causes?

FURTHER READING

George H. Guthrie, *2 Corinthians*, Baker Academic, 2015.

Colin G. Kruse, *2 Corinthians*, IVP, 2015.

Mark A. Seifrid, *The Second Letter to the Corinthians*, Apollos, 2014.

Isaiah 13—39

There are four main sections in Isaiah 13—39. The first eleven chapters (13—23) are a collection of oracles against the nations, such as we find also in other prophetic books (for example, Ezekiel 25—36). A few other items are included here as well, such as material relating to Jerusalem and two prominent city residents in chapter 22, and a short narrative about Isaiah in chapter 20. Nonetheless, these oracles, some of which were certainly written or at least edited after Isaiah's time, clearly show that Isaiah claimed universal sovereignty for his God.

That is probably why this section is followed by chapters that have a global perspective (chs 24—27). They sometimes take up things said about an individual nation and apply them more broadly. Though seemingly referring to the future, they may be better treated as viewing the earth from a heavenly perspective—a way of getting us to see present realities from a completely different angle.

Chapters 28—35 are a varied collection of prophetic oracles. Many obviously relate to the circumstances in the later part of Isaiah's ministry, when he condemned Hezekiah's policy of forming an alliance to oppose the might of the Assyrian empire. Against such frenetic activity, which was accompanied by morally reprehensible behaviour, Isaiah urged a more discreet way of life, based on quiet trust in God and just treatment of all people. Some later oracles are included towards the end of this section, which turn our attention forward, towards the later promise of deliverance in chapters 40—55. Whatever Isaiah himself anticipated, we inevitably see in this final presentation a reflection of the later fall of Judah to the Babylonians, its exile and subsequent restoration.

Finally, chapters 36—39, which are mainly drawn from 2 Kings 18—20, recount the inevitable invasion by Sennacherib that Hezekiah's policy triggered (in 701BC), showing Isaiah's role in that and some related incidents. These chapters, too, end with a clear anticipation of the Babylonian exile (39:6–7).

We have very varied material here to study, and part of our task will be to see if we can trace some underlying theological principles that help to unite them.

Comments are based on the New Revised Standard Version of the Bible.

1 How you are fallen

Isaiah 14:3–21

The first nation to be addressed is Babylon. Two poems (13:2–22; 14:4–21) are joined together by the heading in 13:1, the connecting prose material in 14:1–3, and a conclusion in 14:22–23. Although Babylon is hardly mentioned in the poems themselves, these linking sections make the point clearly: Babylon's eventual fall will lead to the restoration of God's people. Whatever the origins of this material, we can imagine that its message, long after Isaiah's own lifetime, would have encouraged the Judean exiles in Babylon to whom chapters 40—48 seem to be especially addressed, in words which are very close to 14:1–2.

The first poem concerns the overthrow of Babylon as a whole (see 13:19). The second, which is today's passage, focuses on an unidentified 'oppressor' (v. 4), introduced as 'the king of Babylon'. The language is allusive, and it is probable that an older poem has been reused for this new setting. The reference to a character who does not receive proper burial after a battle (vv. 18–20) has led many to think that it may first have been written about the earlier Assyrian king, Sargon II, who died in 705BC. We are used to this recycling of striking expressions. 'The evil empire', for instance, has entered our language and can now be used with reference to whatever global power we may disapprove of, regardless of its original referent.

The deceased king of Babylon is depicted entering the afterlife, Sheol, to a chorus of sarcastic mockery from those he formerly dominated (vv. 9–11). Then follows a colourful description of how he thought he was the equal of God, the Most High, taking titles to himself to match this overweening arrogance: 'Day Star, son of Dawn' (vv. 12–14). His fall will be as ignominious as his ascent was unjustified (vv. 15–20a), providing a lesson for all who would follow his example (vv. 20b–21).

This passage used to be interpreted by some with reference to the primordial fall of Satan. That cannot be justified at the primary level, of course, but it shows how such poetry can be reapplied in many different situations. While we admire the literary genius that has penned so memorable a passage, we should also take the theological principles on which it rests very seriously. Any human pride or hubris, whether individual, corporate, or national, which arrogates to itself that which is exclusively God's, will never endure.

2 The tent of David

Isaiah 15—16

These chapters conclude with an instructive note that is easily over-looked. Isaiah 16:13–14 explicitly makes the point that God's previous prophetic words about Moab need to be updated with a further oracle. Furthermore, parts of these chapters reappear in altered form in Jeremiah 48. Those responsible for bringing us these biblical texts were clearly conscious of the need not just to preserve material out of a respect for antiquity but also to ensure that it was interpreted to serve ongoing needs in changing circumstances—an example that we continue to follow.

That task is not made any easier by the obscurity of much that is said. Moab lay across the Dead Sea to the east of Judah, and the two nations had a chequered relationship. Their frequent conflicts need to be balanced by the recognition that they were relatives (certainly sharing much from cultural and social points of view), so, for example, the story of Ruth the Moabitess can reflect a very different atmosphere.

The bulk of these chapters describes the painful after-effects, whether environmental, emotional, religious or political, of a severe defeat (15:1–9; 16:6–12). The writer seems moved to genuine pity (15:5; 16:9, 11). While many of the details, such as some of the place names, remain obscure, and we do not even know whether the passage describes a real situation or is purely imaginative, it is difficult not to feel the sympathy that the disaster evokes. At the same time, it is noteworthy that pride again lies at the root of the problem (16:6).

Into this elegy, 16:1–5 inserts a strikingly different response. First, the fleeing Moabites should be offered refuge—in Judah, of all places. This will have been a challenge to the Judeans (as its equivalent situations are to us today), inviting an openhearted humanitarian response to appalling distress. The need to 'grant justice' and 'hide the outcasts' should override self-interest and prejudice.

Second, this becomes the basis for a somewhat neglected messianic oracle (16:5). In an unusual image, David's throne will be found in a tent (referring, perhaps, to his priestly character?), but, as in earlier messianic oracles (9:6–7; 11:1–5), the new ruler's role will be to seek justice and righteousness. He will do so with the leavening qualities of steadfast love and faithfulness, so that, to quote a well-known hymn, 'in the darkest spot of earth some love is found'.

3 Called to weeping

Isaiah 22:1–14

As we read through this initially opaque section, it becomes clear that the city is Jerusalem. Care has been taken to prepare for its defence (vv. 8–11), and, despite the initial setback of desertion by some of its leaders (v. 3), it has been dramatically delivered, so that the people are rejoicing exuberantly (vv. 2, 13). All this fits with the invasion by the Assyrian King Sennacherib in 701BC, when he came to put down the rebellion that Hezekiah had initiated.

Isaiah himself, however, could not be more contrary. First, the defences were built at the expense of the houses of the common people who had settled outside the previous walls (v. 10); but public works, especially if undertaken to shore up a political position that should never have been adopted in the first place (rebellion that was not God's will, v. 11), can brook no opposition.

Second, this rejoicing is unseemly because it is based on a short-term perspective (v. 13). Despite the fact that the country was devastated by the invasion and Jerusalem escaped only by the skin of its teeth, the people have not taken the episode as a warning that they need to repent and change their behaviour (vv. 12, 14). They have ignored the lessons that Isaiah tried to teach them through his long lifetime of ministry, so that now, in what may have been one of the last of his oracles, he finds himself isolated and weeping at his apparent failure (v. 4).

Finally, against the people's narrow perspective, Isaiah can see that eventually their unrepentant attitude will lead to their ruin, and this may be reflected in the more apocalyptic sounding verse 5, a verse whose poetic form of expression has given rise to the mysterious title of the passage ('the valley of vision'). So, in addition to the unusual fact that we have an oracle against Isaiah's own people in what is otherwise a collection of oracles against foreign nations, it is introduced and developed in a way that lifts the message out of the woodenly historical. It draws us to reflect on how some of the same principles that Isaiah advocated, despite being constantly ignored, may be ones that we too should heed. Concentration on present prosperity is not always the best perspective.

4   A chaos of emotions

Isaiah 24

After eleven chapters of oracles against specific nations, we move in chapters 24—27 to a collection of material that deals with the world, as well as an unnamed city, in a wider manner. Only with chapter 28 do we return to the more familiar style of oracle.

Several features give us some sense of orientation. First, the language is highly poetic, with many plays on words and sounds that are difficult to capture in an English translation. They create the effect of impressionism rather than detailed depiction.

Second, there are many allusions to and even quotations from elsewhere in the prophets. For instance, compare verses 17–18 with Jeremiah 48:43–44, verse 20b with Amos 5:2, and verses 2 and 4 with Hosea 4:9 and 3. The difference is that, in each case, words originally applied to a specific place or situation are 'universalised' to apply to the whole world.

Third, it follows from this that these chapters were probably written long after the time of Isaiah himself and were put into their present setting to widen the narrow concerns of the oracles against individual nations to universal proportions. What is more, the description seems to turn towards the last days, with its depiction of universal chaos that applies to everyone indiscriminately (vv. 1–4) because they have broken the 'everlasting covenant' (vv. 5–9) that God made with all of humankind in the days of Noah (Genesis 9:8–17).

The responses are very mixed. God is universally praised for his majesty (vv. 14–15), yet the writer is traumatised by the scale of the disaster and the breakdown of civilised society, which, again, will be universal (vv. 16–20).

The conclusion in verses 21–23 reminds us that this contrast with anything previously experienced points to the reality of the differences between the heavenly and earthly realms. The point of all this exaggeration is not to say that we can ignore it because it lies in the distant future but, rather, that we must learn to read our present mundane circumstances against the backdrop of God's perspective. As with all apocalyptic writing, the purpose is not stargazing or an invitation to calculate a timetable for future events; rather, it is a powerful tool to bring us to our senses about true priorities and urge us to respond accordingly.

5 Peace, perfect peace

Isaiah 26:1–19

Chapters 24—27 are punctuated by hymns of praise, and there is one such here in verses 1–6 (see previously 25:1–5). Despite the devastation that characterised chapter 24, the poet maintains that there is one city, presumably Jerusalem/Zion, which does not come into the category of the rejected city elsewhere. Joining with fellow believers, he anticipates the day when it will be open to all who come in good faith, assured that their trust will lead them to find the peace (v. 3) that the world otherwise denies. The proud and the oppressive will be brought low, and we are invited to join in thanksgiving in anticipation of that day.

It is all very attractive, but is it realistic? Following a proverb that asserts the same confidence (v. 7), we are led into a prayer in four sections that debates precisely this conundrum. We may not be used to prayers of this kind, but to debate these real questions before God is spiritually healthy, indicating a mature relationship with him that breathes a greater honesty than is sometimes thought proper.

First, we acknowledge that the hope is not a current experience (vv. 8–9); we are in a period of waiting whose outcome remains undetermined. Second, the present reality is that of the wicked continuing in ignorance of or blindness towards divine realities (vv. 10–11), even if that is not what we could have wished. Rather, third, we maintain our confidence in God (vv. 12–15): we have known (and presumably still know) 'other lords', but we persist in the belief that their time is limited and that God's peace and glory will ultimately prevail.

Finally, however, the tension between the present painful reality and the expectation of faith becomes unbearable (vv. 16–19), like a woman in the pangs of childbirth whose labour brings forth nothing but wind and whose struggles win no victories. To such despair, there comes the extraordinary promise of resurrection like refreshing dew and the restoration of the long-departed shades. It may be that, in this passage, the thought is of national rather than individual resurrection, but the one implies a recognition of the other. The Old Testament here, on one of very few occasions, makes a step of faith towards the conviction that God's truths are eternal and our confidence in him should not be limited to what we see in this world.

6 On that day

Isaiah 27

In the last chapter of this section of Isaiah, we find our attention constantly directed towards the future, with each of its five sections introduced by the phrase 'On that day' or an equivalent.

What a topsy-turvy day that will be! Verse 1 harks back to an ancient myth with which the first readers would have been familiar (some of the wording is more or less identical to a text from the Syrian city of Ugarit, almost a thousand years previously). The archetypical monster, Leviathan, will finally be overthrown (compare Revelation 20:2–3).

Then, equally extraordinarily, verses 2–5 pick up the song of the vineyard from 5:1–7. Whereas there it depicted God's devastating judgement of his people, here the judgement is reversed: the 'thorns and briers' that he sent then to overrun the vineyard will now, in turn, be burned up.

A longer, slightly more complex section follows in verses 6–11, although reversal of previous or even present judgement is again the unifying factor. This is clear in the introductory verse 6 (contrast 5:24). The following verses recall times of defeat and exile and the emptiness of unsanctioned religious practices, all of which will be overturned. Finally, the city depicted several times in the previous chapters reappears in verses 10–11, now deserted and no longer a source of irresistible temptation.

The last two verses are both introduced by 'On that day' as they depict the ingathering of the dispersed people, whether they be within the borders of the land (v. 12) or outside it (v. 13). The climax is that the people's return becomes a great act of pilgrimage and worship at God's appointed sanctuary.

Thus, through diverse imagery and the initially intimidating portrayal of a universal cataclysm, chapters 24—27 come to a conclusion with a varied assurance that even such threats will not be God's last word. It is difficult to see how this language can be related directly to the world of international politicking that began back in chapter 13, but, if faith cannot hold on to the assurance of God's ultimate control even through the darkest and most hopeless of circumstances, then it is vain. The world's 'fortified city' (v. 10) will not outlast the city of God.

Guidelines

Christians react in diverse ways to news of international affairs. At one extreme, some say that we are 'not of this world', and that nationalism and politics are nothing more than a reflection of a sinful and doomed humanity; it is not our place to get involved. At the other extreme, some argue that Christ calls us to get involved with the world at its messiest, and that the most meaningful expression of discipleship is to try to work within the systems that exist, in the interests of justice and compassion. Perhaps most of us sit firmly in the middle—with a few well-sounding prayers, a donation to some good charities that work on behalf of us all, and a shake of the head over the intractability of the problems.

Isaiah 13—27 will not solve these differences but these chapters perhaps include some additional perspectives to goad us in our thinking. They bring a prophetic focus to bear on specific nations and situations as initially they seek to discern the overarching theological principles that govern the nations' and their leaders' actions. Then, in chapters 24—27, they track all this to an even higher level of abstraction in apocalyptic language that urges us to view the present in terms of its heavenly and eternal counterpart. This tends to level the differences between national, community and individual behaviour, so that, however we react to the news (and that is a decision for each to make on their own), we should also reflect on the extent to which those matters we most readily condemn or applaud in others may also be apparent in our own lives, and respond appropriately.

1 A precious cornerstone

Isaiah 28:1–19

The opening verses bring us one final oracle against a nation. It is the nation of Ephraim, Isaiah's usual name for the northern kingdom of Israel, which fell to the Assyrians in 721BC. Although there is potential hope even for them (vv. 5–6), they are depicted with withering scorn as drunk, overfed and dressed with fading floral garlands, a symbol of their self-satisfied pride. It is a tawdry scene, like the debris in a room the day after a rowdy party.

God's announcement of their violent demise would have roused the southern Judean crowds to cheer, of course. And, just like the rhetoric in Amos 1—2, that is its purpose, for Isaiah now goes on to show how they are thereby condemning themselves. By verse 14, we know that he is talking about Jerusalem. In fact, he starts to do so subtly, almost ambiguously, at verse 7. The religious leaders, who more recently have been urging the nation to form foreign alliances against Assyria, even though Isaiah warned in God's name that this was a foolish course of action, are themselves acting like drunkards. In their stupor they mock Isaiah's teaching as infantile (vv. 9–10), but he retorts that they will be taught eventually not just by him but by the very foreigners whom they think they are capable of resisting (vv. 11–13).

In a phrase whose precise meaning is disputed, Isaiah then categorises their political schemes, which they think will protect them, as a 'covenant with death' (vv. 14–15). His warning includes, at least, the notion that it will turn into a self-defeating course of action, certain to fail (vv. 18–19).

The contrast, which Isaiah continues to maintain, is a sure trust in God that does not give place to frantic but blinkered human scheming. He presents such trust through the picture of a building that has secure foundations and well-aligned walls (see also 1 Peter 2:6). The test of its security is an adherence to that radical social justice which he so often characterises as justice and righteousness (vv. 16–17).

Our circumstances today are very different, of course, but we may still carefully reflect on the contrast that this chapter presents—adherence to divinely revealed principles by which we can safely orientate our life and outlook, or self-deluding confidence in our own schemes and abilities which will bring us nothing better than stumbling in 'filthy vomit'.

2 A rebellious people

Isaiah 30:1–18

Today's passage clarifies some of the issues that were rather veiled in yesterday's. Perhaps time has moved on, so that now the Assyrian invasion is imminent and Isaiah makes one last desperate attempt to bring his people to their senses.

First, it is made explicit that the attempt to forge an alliance with Egypt is misguided and in vain (vv. 1–5). Presumably that might not always have been the case, but on this occasion it most certainly is. It is not God's plan; indeed it is against his will. The people think that Pharaoh will be their 'protection' and 'shelter', terms that their liturgy in the Psalms should have taught them are God's own prerogative. The cause of the condemnation is, therefore, a mistaken confusion of the human and the divine. Their diplomatic mission is nicely satirised as costly and dangerous, in pursuit of something useless (vv. 6–7).

Then comes a theologically fundamental passage in the book. God's word may be rejected by rebellious contemporaries, but it cannot ultimately be thwarted. In 8:16–17, Isaiah committed his words to writing in the expectation that he would live to see the change from judgement to deliverance. Now, some 30 years later, he realises that this will not happen, so his words must be committed to writing again—this time, however, as a witness to what God has said for some more distant future (v. 8). The judgement to come is not arbitrary or mistaken. Future readers will know that it was because the people rejected this word of trust in place of alliances (v. 15); note, for instance, how the building in 28:16–17 is now out of alignment and ready to collapse (v. 13). So, when deliverance eventually comes, readers will learn not to repeat the mistakes of the past.

That principle might have applied at various times, but it would have resonated especially with those who were offered deliverance from exile in Babylon in the second half of the book. The existence of the written word resonates long after any single specific incident. The passage ends in verse 18 with a broader assurance that God is ultimately gracious and merciful and that he will not disappoint any who wait expectantly for him, whether in ancient times or modern.

3 The ideal king

Isaiah 32

The first verse is a proverb rather than a prediction, meaning 'a king should reign to further righteousness, and princes should rule to further justice' (compare Proverbs 8:15–16). It is not, therefore, a messianic prophecy in the traditional sense. Nevertheless, it encapsulates the ideal of rule from God's perspective, which applies not just to kings but also to all in authority (the so-called 'princes'). Of course, the ideal is one with which we are familiar from related passages in Isaiah, notably 9:2–7 and 11:1–5. The application will vary according to circumstances, however. In Isaiah's time, there were certainly many transgressions against justice at the most blatant level (for example, 1:21–23; 3:13–15), and it was the duty of the king to ensure that they did not continue.

In our day, whether internationally, in the national and political spheres, or even within the church and family life, the circumstances are very different and we each have a responsibility to think through the way this underlying principle should be worked out. Positions of authority carry primary responsibilities towards others, not a mandate for self-perpetuation. What is certain, however, is that here, as elsewhere, we have in Jesus the perfect embodiment and expression of what it meant in his circumstances—as a prophet and teacher living under all the restrictions of occupation by a foreign power. In that sense, the verse can indeed be labelled 'messianic'; equally, we must admit that we cannot escape its demand simply because our social circumstances differ from Isaiah's.

The remainder of the chapter does not really need commentary. It is better read through thoughtfully with the guiding principle of verse 1 in mind, to see how it evokes supportive images to inspire imitation, and signs that warn us to take care. Verses 16 and 17 return to the opening theme, but they arrive there by way of both pastoral and urban images, as well as through intellectual and gender distinctions, in a manner that evokes longing for improvement as well as incentive to avoid neglect. The availability of the 'spirit from on high' (v. 15) reminds us that we are not left to do this by our own devices; we act in dependence on the God who inspired the vision, and in harmony with the way in which he desires to see his creation being ordered.

4 Everlasting joy

Isaiah 35

This is the last poetic passage in the first half of the book before we come to the narratives that round it off in a completely different style. It is a passage of positive and unalloyed joy, which sounds like parts of chapters 40—55; indeed, verse 10 is identical to 51:11, and close parallels with other elements in the chapter could fill all of today's comments.

Given these similarities, why does it need to appear here at all? The answer probably is that the editors of the book wanted to record all the blood and thunder of Isaiah's early invective against his people, to explain why disaster had befallen them and to warn later readers to learn from their sorry history, but they also wanted to make clear that judgement was not God's last word. Elements of hope sit alongside the words of judgement, a pattern reflected in the way that the entire book has been shaped, with the second half as a whole bespeaking imminent salvation and deliverance. Similarly, chapter 12 was a hymn of praise to conclude the first large section of the book, and chapter 35 serves the same purpose at the close of this next major section.

There is no reason to be shy about the exuberant form of praise that we find here. Some have tried to deaden its force by arguing, for instance, that the theme of the desert blossoming like a rose (or, rather, crocus) has been fulfilled literally in recent decades by the agricultural development of the Negev. That, however, completely misses the point; we cannot select one element and treat it in isolation. Rather, we must allow the poetry that envisages the transformation of the desert, of the wild animals, and of those who are disabled either physically, spiritually or emotionally, to grip our imagination and encourage us on the no less metaphorical highway that God has prepared for his people (v. 8; for those who are cartographically challenged, it is reassuring to read that not even fools will go astray!).

In religious worship, hymns, psalms and spiritual songs are sometimes equally pictorial. While I am the last person to dismiss the need for honest, sober, intellectual engagement with the Bible and with our faith, of equal legitimacy is an emotional response to the personal love and faithfulness of a God who delivers in spite of every failure and weakness.

5 'The Assyrian came down'

Isaiah 37:1–7, 21–29, 36–38

Chapters 36—39 are close to 2 Kings 18—20. They recount the invasion of Sennacherib in 701BC to put down the rebellion by a coalition of states with Hezekiah as a ringleader. An editor of Isaiah has probably taken this material from 2 Kings. Even though there are links with other material in Isaiah, the presentation of the prophet himself is different from what we have seen elsewhere. Usually he is critical of anything to do with the rebellion, whereas in these chapters he appears as a strong supporter of the king now that the issue has come to the crunch.

We know from many sources that Judah was devastated but, for some reason, Jerusalem itself was eventually spared and Hezekiah was allowed to continue his reign. Two accounts of this unusual outcome seem to have been combined, and today's verses have been selected to highlight that combination. Verses 1–7, reflecting one account, tell how Isaiah predicted that the blockade would be lifted because a rumour would send Sennacherib hurrying home, and that he would be assassinated there. This prediction is fulfilled in verses 37–38, even though, historically, Sennacherib's violent death occurred 20 years later. In the other account (vv. 33–36), Jerusalem is saved by a miraculous intervention that swiftly wipes out the bulk of the Assyrian army. Even if we postulate sudden disease or the like, the numbers involved and the manner of narrative clearly transcend the bounds of normal historical writing.

The rest of the material in chapters 36—37 shows that we also have two accounts of messengers being sent by Sennacherib to try to get Jerusalem to surrender (ch. 36; 37:9–13). Then, in verses 21–29 we have

Isaiah's magnificent response. He quotes some of Sennacherib's boasts about his conquests (vv. 23–25) and claims that these were due only to God's wider purposes (vv. 26–27). Because Sennacherib has claimed that they were his own achievements, his arrogance will be met by eventual ignominy (vv. 28–29), allowing the citizens of Zion to mock him as once he did them (v. 22).

All this is quite similar to the ways in which Isaiah previously condemned the Judeans, and that is perhaps the main lesson to be drawn from this material, despite the historical uncertainties. God's principles are unchanging and are applied equally to friend and foe. God has no favourites; we are all alike in our guilt before him and in our dependence on his undifferentiated mercy.

6 Hezekiah's sickness

Isaiah 38

Just like 2 Kings 20, chapters 38 and 39 relate two incidents that are associated with Sennacherib's invasion, although the events probably took place before it. Chapter 39 is best understood as part of the preparations of the anti-Assyrian coalition through negotiation with the Babylonians. In judgement for this, Isaiah predicts that one day Hezekiah's descendants will be exiled to Babylon. This makes for a good transition to the next major section of the book (chs 40—48), which presupposes precisely this time and place of exile.

Isaiah 38:6 shows that the account of Hezekiah's sickness also preceded Sennacherib's invasion. Perhaps its main point is that the king experienced a severe threat to his own life, just as the nation's life would soon be threatened, and that through prayer and the intervention of the prophet he was delivered. It thus helps us to see how the theological principles in the nation's life also work out at the individual level.

The particularly distinctive feature of this chapter is the inclusion of Hezekiah's psalm-like prayer in verses 9–20. This is the one extensive element in all these chapters that does not also appear in 2 Kings, so it deserves attention.

Like many psalms, it starts with a description of a state of distress (vv. 10–12). It does so in words that do not say much about Hezekiah's specific ailment, suggesting that the kind of language used can be applied by each reader to her or his own problems. We can equally well identify with the desperation that leads us to 'cry for help until morning'. Hezekiah belabours the intensity of his prayer, born out of distress (vv. 13–14). Then (in verses 15–17, which are difficult to translate in places), he affirms that God has responded to his prayer by snatching him back from the brink of 'the pit'. Finally (vv. 18–20), he lifts his vision to encompass his contemporaries and his successors in a commitment to the public worship of God.

The prayer thus helps to put all Isaiah's teaching into true perspective: whether in danger or in deliverance, we do not live and experience spiritual realities in isolation. Our understanding can be shared with others in testimony as we encourage one another to join together in the higher calling of worship.

Guidelines

How should we respond to the variety of material that we have been studying? At one level, we have seen some themes that help to unite it. Isaiah and his editors clearly saw and interpreted their world from a broadly united theological standpoint. At the same time, however, they committed it to writing for the benefit of later generations (30:8) with the unspoken assumption that they—and we too—would work out how those principles should be fitted to developing circumstances.

Their ultimate purpose, however, was not just intellectual. Understanding rooted in faith led them to praise and worship, as we saw in both chapters 35 and 38. In part, that worship might have been personal and private, but, as presented here, it was corporate—or, should we say, congregational. Our study should not remain only personal but should also transform our worship when we are with fellow believers. Let us pray, therefore, that our studies may lead to the enhancement of our church's worship as we share with others some of the insights we have gained from Isaiah.

FURTHER READING

John Barton, *Isaiah 1—39* (T&T Clark Study Guides), T&T Clark, 2003

John Goldingay, *Isaiah* (New International Biblical Commentary), Hendrickson/ Paternoster, 2001

Christopher Seitz, *Isaiah 1—39* (Interpretation), John Knox Press, 1993

Patricia K. Tull, *Isaiah 1—39* (Smyth & Helwys Bible Commentary), Smyth & Helwys, 2010

The spirituality of motherhood

In Western culture in the early 21st century, we find ourselves reluctant to talk about motherhood. There is a host of motives behind this reticence—some good, some not so good. Rightly, we are sensitive to those who cannot be (biological) mothers, whether through singleness, relationship breakdown, health issues or failed IVF. We are also aware of the half of the population who are male: after all, the renaissance in fatherhood is surely good news.

In an age striving for sexual equality, it is encouraging to see so many women flourishing and reaching their potential in the workplace, opening many doors that were closed to our grandmothers. However, perhaps the quest for unnuanced equality sometimes overshadows the gift of motherhood. Mary Sumner, founder of the Mothers' Union, offers some wise words in her principles—for example, that 'the prosperity of a nation springs from the family life of the homes'. The UK has one of the highest rates of family breakdown in Europe.

These are complex topics. They can leave our 'spiritual compasses' in a spin, tempting us to play safe and leave motherhood alone, but this is not an option. We believe in a God who did not leave motherhood alone, but chose an unlikely mother for his Son's gestation, birth and parenting until his early death.

This week, as we approach Christmas Day, we will be reflecting on the spirituality of motherhood. We take Mary as our compass—her favour, expectancy, pain, fragility and wonder. Some parts of the church have played safe and, by and large, left Mary alone; but again this is not an option for us if we want to enjoy Christmas refreshed by the scriptures. Each day's reading from Luke's Gospel closes with a spiritual reflection for all who wait with expectancy for the Christ-child to 'be born in us again'.

Quotations are taken from the New International Version of the Bible.

1 Favoured

Luke 1:26–38

What astonishing words from the angel (v. 28): 'Greetings, you who are highly favoured! The Lord is with you.'

What does it mean to be 'highly favoured'? To become the 'mother of my Lord' (to quote Elizabeth in Luke 1:43) was an immense, epoch-changing privilege. The 13th-century mystic Julian of Norwich describes how she asked for a vision of Mary, and in the vision Mary's face was radiant with her simple acceptance of God's favour: 'Can you see in her how greatly you are loved?' (*Revelations of Divine Love*, 25). Mary accepted God's favour with a simple 'yes'—'May your word to me be fulfilled' (v. 38)—and an incredible train of events ensued.

Mary was an unlikely choice for the 'mother of my Lord'. It seems that God does not bestow his favour as we might advise him to; and, indeed, accepting God's favour is not as straightforward as we might think. Fast-forward in Luke's Gospel to Jesus' famous story of the prodigal son and see the elder son's furrowed brow as he wrestles with his father's response to his complaint about the favour showered on the delinquent younger brother: 'Everything I have is yours' (15:31). Henri Nouwen, in *The Return of the Prodigal Son*, accurately diagnoses that there is an elder son in all of us, who is so distracted by God's seemingly indiscriminate favour on others that he misses the favour in his own life.

For the vast majority of women, becoming a mum means becoming one who is favoured. One is deeply conscious of those who would love to conceive or even just to find the life partner with whom they might one day conceive.

Advent is a time of getting ready. May we be ready for God's favour. Are our hearts open wide enough in trust to receive all God's favour on our lives? Do we find it hard to imagine a God who patiently reasons with us while we are grumbling in the fields? Listen to him now. Hear his words today: 'I tell you, now is the time of God's favour' (2 Corinthians 6:2).

2 Expectancy

'We are expecting' is an ever-so-politically-correct way of describing pregnancy. What are you expecting? This is a timely question for the end of Advent in the context of motherhood. Children continually defy expectations. In pregnancy it's impossible to imagine their character, looks and talents. In fact, it can be damaging to a child when particular expectations are placed on their slight shoulders. My own mother was a disappointment from birth because her father was expecting a long-awaited boy.

With God, however, we would do well to cultivate an attitude of *expectancy*, while sitting light to our *expectations*. We have a God 'who is able to do immeasurably more than all we ask or imagine' (Ephesians 3:20), and he is in the business of surpassing expectations.

Mary was asked to have faith in a way that was without precedent, surpassing any expectations. It was not just faith that a battle would be won, land conquered or even a dead person raised. She was asked to have faith in the absolutely impossible, something that had never happened before in the history of the universe—the incarnation. 'You will conceive and give birth to a son, and you are to call him Jesus. He will be great and will be called the Son of the Most High… He will reign… for ever; his kingdom will never end' (vv. 31–33).

Mary has such a simple, face-value response of trust (v. 38): 'May your word to me be fulfilled.' Have you noticed how Luke contrasts Mary's response with Zechariah's, earlier in the chapter? Zechariah's response to the angel was, 'How can I be sure of this?' (1:18). A friend of mine says that it's like a slap in the face to God when we don't trust him. Have you ever worked (or lived) with someone who didn't trust you? It's exhausting and dehumanising.

During this week before Christmas, may we cultivate a culture of faith and expectancy. What impossible vision is God asking you to have faith in? The Holy Spirit is longing to conceive his visions, his new life in us. He is just looking for people like Mary who will quite simply say 'Yes'. Because these visions are divine, of course they're impossible! But he can do 'immeasurably more than all we ask or imagine'. 'Blessed is she who has believed that the Lord would fulfil his promises to her' (1:45).

3 Hiddenness

Luke 1:38–56

The spiritual discipline of hiddenness echoes through the lives of the heroes of faith. Moses, David, Paul and even Jesus all spent time in the wilderness. Perhaps this was essential to their character formation, enabling them to withstand the demands of their ultimate calling under God.

It's very striking that Mary's instinctive response to the angel's epoch-shattering news is to spend three months hidden away in an unnamed town in the hill country of Judea (vv. 39, 56). In this hidden place she digests her precious news in private, after it has been coaxed out by the revelation given to Elizabeth by the Holy Spirit (1:41–45).

Motherhood is an intrinsically hidden calling. The baby is 'made in the secret place... woven together in the depths of the earth' (Psalm 139:13–15); then, the significant moments of mothering children happen when no one is looking.

Hiddenness is not in vogue in our social media culture, with its relentless demand to prove that something important is happening and that we are at the centre of it. In contrast, hiddenness is often the way of God. In nature, seeds germinate in the darkness, and many international church growth movements are happening out of the media spotlight of Western Europe, in the hidden places of South America, Africa and Asia. As Jackie Pullinger once said, 'If you want your church to grow, plant it in the gutter.'

Mary's motherhood has many resonances with God's hidden way of working, captured by Luke in the famous Magnificat (1:46–55), 'He has... lifted up the humble. He has filled the hungry with good things.' From start to finish, the arrival of God on earth is hidden: 'How silently, how silently the wondrous gift is given,' says the Christmas hymn, and Isaiah 30:15 tells us, 'In quietness and trust is your strength.'

Mary did not journey alone. Elizabeth brought a beautiful gift to her cousin, in recognising and sharing her joy. Do you have a friend like this? Do you have a friend who draws out from you the hidden hopes and fears and notices the work of God in your life? Perhaps you might resolve to spend some hidden time receiving encouragement from such a friend or mentor. Out of these hidden times can emerge fresh perspectives, more daring expectancy and the most wonderful Magnificats.

4 Fragility

Luke 2:1–18

There can be an instinctive assumption that if, like Mary, we say 'yes' to God's impossible visions, then it will all be plain sailing, but this is not Mary's story. I am continually astonished by the fragility of God's plan.

After returning from the hill country of Judea, amid suspicions of infidelity to her fiancé, she had to travel the 70–80 miles from Nazareth to Bethlehem, heavily pregnant. We might think that, on her arrival, the 'power of the Most High' (1:35) would have arranged a suitable maternity suite for the birth of the Son of God. Instead it appears that Mary and Joseph were left scrabbling around for accommodation, and tradition has it that she delivered her baby in a stable. Then things deteriorated further: King Herod got wind of a challenge to his throne and the family had to flee in the night to Egypt (Matthew 2:13–14). My experience is that this pattern is typical of the way many things come to birth in the divine economy: your friends are suspicious and your enemies want to kill the 'baby'.

Why this fragility? The early days of birth and motherhood can be an especially precarious time. This is a pattern observed by Julian of Norwich in creation itself. Famously, she had a vision of 'a little thing, the quantity of a hazelnut, lying in the palm of my hand'. Julian writes:

I thought, 'What may this be?' And it was answered generally thus: 'It is all that is made.' I wondered how it could last, for I thought it might suddenly fall to nothing for little cause. And I was answered in my understanding: 'It lasts and ever shall, for God loves it; and so everything has its beginning by the love of God.' (Revelations of Divine Love, Ch. V)

Yet in the midst of this fragility, there is peace. Mary has some unlikely visitors: wide-eyed shepherds appear at the stable door, looking for a baby in a manger, bringing tales of angelic hosts. Crazily they confirm Gabriel's message from nine months previously, and again they talk of favour: 'on earth peace to those on whom his favour rests' (2:14).

The Christmas cards that adorn our homes often carry the phrase 'peace on earth'. Where would you like to see God's peace today? Welcome the Prince of Peace: 'Of the greatness of his government and peace there will be no end' (Isaiah 9:7).

5 Pain

Luke 2:22–40

Today we reflect on this beautiful account of Mary and Joseph meeting Simeon and Anna in the temple, where the vision for Mary's baby is marvellously reiterated and again enlarged: he is to be 'a light for revelation to the Gentiles, and the glory of your people Israel' (v. 32). There is so much epoch-changing hope here, and yet Simeon sounds a painful note in his prophecy: 'This child is destined to cause the falling and rising of many in Israel, and to be a sign that will be spoken against, so that the thoughts of many hearts will be revealed. And a sword will pierce your own soul too' (2:34–35). What devastating news to a young mum on a special day! Perhaps it was necessary to prepare Mary for the cost of being the 'mother of our Lord'.

Motherhood is inherently painful. Few women go through the early days of childbirth and sleepless nights without experiencing physical pain at a level never experienced before. Later, as the child grows, there is the inevitable pain of separation and loss as they rightly find their feet in the world.

One way I like to relax is to compile photos for our family albums. I am conscious that I never include photos of the tantrums, the disappointments or the stress of missing the ferry on the way home from holiday. There were many painful stories in Mary's family album: losing the twelve-year-old Jesus in Jerusalem for three days (Luke 2:41–46); losing him to the Galilean crowds (8:19–21); seemingly being disowned by him (11:27–28); and, most agonisingly, losing him to death on the cross (John 19:25–27).

There is a strand in the New Testament that, in some mysterious way, we are called to share in Jesus' sufferings. Paul writes to 'my dear children, for whom I am again in the pains of childbirth until Christ is formed in you' (Galatians 4:19; see also Philippians 3:10–11; Colossians 1:24; 2 Corinthians 1:5). This strand is movingly highlighted in the writings of mystics such as Teresa of Avila and St John of the Cross.

Mary was called to share in the sufferings of Jesus. The centurion's sword pierced Jesus' side, and Simeon correctly prophesied that a sword would pierce her own soul too. Where can you see the sufferings of Jesus in your life? Where is there a sword piercing your soul? Talk to the one who shares your sufferings.

6 Wonder

Luke 2:16–20

Today we return to an earlier passage to draw out our final theme in the spirituality of motherhood: wonder.

I like to think that when Luke the doctor sat down with an elderly Mary as part of his personal quest to 'carefully investigate everything from the beginning' (Luke 1:3), she finally told her story of the incredible things that she had 'treasured up' and 'pondered… in her heart' (2:19). Let's stay with this spirituality of Mary for a moment.

Sometimes new mums are infectiously full of wonder. There is an amazing delight about the first smile, first word, first step and first full night of sleep, and this sense of wonder continues as children grow up. It's this that sustains the most unlikely parent through the ups and downs of the ongoing task. As my brother pithily described his firstborn: 'He's so cute—I wish he'd stop doing that to me.'

What sustained Mary's faith through her risky pregnancy and birth? What fed her soul through the fragility of exile, the pain of the sword piercing her heart, and the bewilderment of seemingly being disowned? I think it was the way she handled God's encouragements and his shafts of light in the darkness: from Gabriel, Elizabeth, the shepherds, Simeon and Anna. There is something very hidden and private about the work of God—to be treasured up and pondered.

My spiritual director often reminds me that thankfulness is a great antidote to fear. Wonder is a precious attitude if we want to build our faith in God. It is a deeply divine discipline: as Proverbs 8:30–31 puts it, 'I was filled with delight day after day, rejoicing always in his presence, rejoicing in his whole world and delighting in the human race.'

What are you treasuring today? Mary had the angel Gabriel's words: what promises have been made to you? Mary had her cousin Elizabeth, who celebrated with her: who has believed your vision? She had the beautiful surprise of the angels and shepherds, and the amazing prophecies of two saints who 'coincidentally' bumped into her in the temple. She treasured up all these things and pondered them in her heart. Take time to wonder and treasure up today.

Guidelines

As we draw together the strands of our journey through the spirituality of motherhood, allow yourself space to reflect on it in the presence of the Spirit. What does he highlight? What have you been drawn to in the past few readings?

- Do we have faith with Mary to say 'Yes' to God's favour and to his impossible visions?
- Do you have a friend like Elizabeth? Is there someone who brings out from you the hidden hopes and fears, and notices the work of God in your life?
- Where would you like to see peace on earth? Do you need to release the weight from your shoulders, in the knowledge and trust that 'the government will be on his shoulders' (Isaiah 9:6)?
- Where can you see the sufferings of Jesus in your life? Where is there a sword piercing your soul?
- Finally, what are you treasuring up today and pondering in your heart to sustain you through the Christmas season?

Motherhood is a precious gift, and so is the gift of Jesus. May we brood deeply over God's immeasurable gifts this Christmas.

Mission and incarnation

Whether we think of Paul's missionary travels or of crossing the road to take a meal to a sick neighbour, mission usually conveys movement. This is hardly surprising, for in scripture we encounter such movement in God's act of approaching his creation.

As an introduction to this study, it will be helpful to read Philippians 2:5–11. Paul's verses trace a wonderful parabolic curve. In this richest of theological passages, the initial focus is ethical. It describes the mindset or attributes we need in relating to one another and, by extension, to the world. The life of Jesus that we see in this passage, as it unfolds, offers us a wonderful, if challenging, template for mission. Jesus begins in a place of equality with his heavenly Father, yet he surrenders that privilege and embarks on a journey of identification with those he seeks to serve and save. Then, having served and saved, he is exalted by the Father to the highest place.

Here, then, is the paradigm for us to follow, but to whom is it applicable? Is it only for so-called missionaries? In fact, the dedication required to live in a strange land, learn a new language, enter into someone else's story and understand their worldview offers us a parallel template that we can apply to our mission here at home as well. I'll be using that template in the readings this week as we also consider the missionary calling to reach out to our next-door neighbours, to sit with them, listen to their stories, learn their 'language' and see the world through their eyes.

Bible quotations are from the New Revised Standard Version unless otherwise stated.

26 December–1 January

1 Gestation

Luke 1:26–45

Ask people when or where 'the Word became flesh' and most will instinctively reply, 'At the birth of Jesus, in Bethlehem.' It's an easy mistake to make, but the right answer is surely 'At the moment of the annunciation, in Nazareth.' When Mary uttered the words 'Let it be with me according to your word' (v. 38), the incarnation of Jesus began to unfold.

This helps us to see an important connection between the *kenosis* mentioned in Philippians 2:7 (he 'emptied himself') and the embryo. The vulnerability of the self-emptying Christ is evidenced first in the womb, only later in the manger and ultimately on the cross. The womb is a place of preparation where the potential of new life is nurtured and brought towards birth.

If Philippians 2:5–11 says something to us about our missionary journey, then the embryo stage is not one we can afford to leave out. Before we undertake the activities that reflect our Christian faith, our missionary calling, there is a need to re-enter the womb and move through a process of preparation. Maybe then we can truly talk of being 'born again'. This womb experience is a time to stop and face the need to let go of all the things that have hitherto defined our identity. Its nearest equivalent is a solitary time of prayerful reflection. I reflect on my own ministry and wonder whether I have encouraged new converts to 'pause and consider' the new life that now confronts them.

If this seems daunting to us (and it should), Mary had a similar concern and was 'much perplexed' (v. 29). If it seems impossible, Mary experienced this feeling too (v. 34). I wonder whether our call to discipleship is challenging enough to trigger these kinds of reactions—in ourselves as well as in those we lead.

Ultimately, it is only the Holy Spirit (v. 35) who can fashion this new birth into a new culture, carrying us into the world of a people who are not 'my people', even if they live across the street from us. We might even dare to say that the new 'I' who emerges from the womb will be a fusion of the person I was, the person I am becoming and the people I have come to serve. Was this not true of the one who was both human and divine?

2 New birth

Luke 2:1–7

It is in the moment of birth that the intentions of God become clear. The choice of a redeemer who comes in glory is rejected; instead, the mission of God towards and among humankind is tangibly expressed in the birth of a child.

In the experience of birth, God demonstrates that mission is a profound act of identification, and is not achieved without cost. Birth is a messy business involving blood, sweat and tears, and all of these were present at the birth of Jesus, with more to follow. I have known many missionaries for whom the early days of their mission were daunting. Nothing quite prepares you for the sights and sounds of a foreign land, the incomprehensibility of the language, and the feeling of not belonging.

The arrival of Jesus was not devoid of a greater context, though. The magnificent genealogy in Matthew 1:1–17 brings home the fact that this birth was the fulfilment of the prophecy given to Abraham. So too, every missionary incarnation is evidence of the continuing mandate to the church: 'As the Father has sent me, so I send you' (John 20:21).

In some measure (often great measure), that 'sending' is characterised by weakness. If we go with due humility, we will accept the need to be held and nursed, nurtured and assisted by the very people we are going to serve. All the skills in the world will not have the same impact as the act of simply going and living with others, learning from them and sharing their life. I have seen many missionaries who failed to learn the language well but were greatly loved because they entered into the life of the people.

We can also be reminded that even Jesus was not universally seen as good news, even as a baby. Mary accepted that this was God's will, but we can be sure that this was not how she had expected to bear her first child. Joseph was deeply troubled too (Matthew 1:19), and Herod would kill many innocents later, in the hope that among them would be this new child (Matthew 2:16). Mission is a delight when it is welcomed, but, even when we have the right attitude and a desire to serve, the privilege is not ours to claim by right.

3 Growing and learning

Luke 2:41–52

To have a glimpse of the childhood of Jesus is an extraordinary gift. In this account, we see a pattern for devout family life (v. 41). It tells us of Jesus' confidence, which led him to stay behind in Jerusalem (v. 43), and it captures well the reaction of his frantic parents who were simultaneously 'anxious' and 'astonished' and puzzled by his behaviour (v. 48). Were they angry or confused or relieved... or all three?

Above all, this passage marks the first known turning point in Jesus' life and ministry. It reveals a clear awareness in him that his life was for a higher purpose, that his heavenly Father was the one who set the direction, and that even his human family had to take second place (Luke 14:26).

Bringing up children is the most important task that parents are never trained to do! But creating a rhythm of family life is one way of sowing the seeds of a faith that will, one day, blossom. It seems obvious that a family who made annual visits to Jerusalem would also have been regular attenders at the local synagogue.

For today's parents, a pattern of prayer established in infancy and continuing around the family table, a familiarity with Bible stories and a consistent charitable attitude towards others can all create an environment in which faith awakens. In this environment, even a child can begin to understand the claims of God upon their life.

Any mission commitment involves an experience of departure, away from that which is familiar and comfortable, towards something less predictable and more costly. That departure, to be authentic, must flow from a relationship with God in which his will is made known, for it is the knowledge of God's will that sustains the believer through hardship and suffering. This is the kind of relationship that, for Jesus, years later, would allow him to cry, 'Yet, not my will but yours be done' (Luke 22:42).

Jesus returned happily to Nazareth, but Mary had seen something, even if she didn't fully understand it yet. A child is never so young that an attentive parent cannot see and treasure the potential of a life made available to God.

4 Maintaining contact

John 1:1–14

There is a danger to consider when we use the image of a journey to describe the way Jesus left the glory of heaven and entered into the earthy reality of human existence. It can convey the idea of a withdrawal from the Father's presence, but nothing could be further from the truth. Jesus lived continually in the consciousness of his relationship with his heavenly Father. Our previous reading showed Jesus at a young age speaking of 'my Father's business' (Luke 2:49, KJV). His later baptism in the Jordan and the voice from heaven, along with his many references to 'my Father in heaven', underline this connection.

In today's reading, we see the same truth on the lips of others. The life, death and resurrection of Jesus made such an impact on his followers that they were able to make the connection themselves—between the Jesus whom 'we have heard… seen with our eyes... and touched with our hands' and the declaration that 'the eternal life that was with the Father… was revealed to us' (1 John 1:1–2).

Notice two things. First, the gospel is a multisensory experience. Here we read of sight, sound and touch. Elsewhere, Paul uses the imagery of fragrance to denote the presence of Christ among his people (2 Corinthians 2:15), and the psalmist encourages us to taste and see that the Lord is good (Psalm 34:8).

An authentic commitment to the gospel will indeed give opportunity for people to *hear* the message, but they will also experience it in many other ways. Never let it be said again that the practical expressions of the gospel are secondary. People can hear about God's grace but they also need to feel it (in the touch of a caring hand), taste it (in the practical provision of a meal), smell it (in the recognition that they are not being judged) and see it (in the person who is physically there when needed).

Second, missionary Christians are often activists. They see a need and they get stuck in, work long hours and expend huge amounts of energy. If we become detached from the Father, however, the oxygen of faith runs out and we are left merely with our human endeavours. Our commitment to mission must not become an excuse to allow our relationship with our heavenly Father to dry up. People will remember their experience of the gospel in us—or its absence—long after they have forgotten what we said.

5 The costliness of love

John 13:1–30

This was no ordinary meal. The disciples had gathered and so had the storm clouds. There was a breathtaking demonstration of servant leadership but also a sense of foreboding (v. 1). One of his friends was about to betray him and this left Jesus deeply troubled (v. 21). Peter asked 'the one whom Jesus loved' (v. 23), possibly John himself, to seek clarification, and Jesus handed the piece of bread to Judas.

'For God so loved the world...' (John 3:16) reminds us that the primary motivation for mission is love, but love is a costly thing. The rewards are wonderful but the risks of rejection, betrayal, grief and loss are high.

Incarnational mission requires an emotional engagement. Even though love is the foundation, it is not the only emotion that mission evokes. Jesus' love was rejected by a young man who walked away from him (Mark 10:21–22). Jesus showed deep compassion (Matthew 9:36) and profound grief and agitation (Matthew 26:37–38). He was joyful (John 15:11) but also indignant (Mark 10:14) and driven to tears (John 11:35). Incarnational mission propels us into people's lives, where we can be richly blessed but also deeply wounded by the experience.

In spite of this, the best mission workers are those who love the people they serve. A busy Thursday morning in the local Foodbank offers a clue. Here you won't find saints of the otherworldly kind, but you will meet people who are motivated by love and compassion, even if at times they are exasperated and angry. This is sleeves-rolled-up mission, the experience of pain underwritten by love.

Understanding our motivation for mission is of the greatest importance. As a church minister, I felt the pressure to succeed and perhaps monitored too closely the membership numbers. As a mission leader, I know the pressure to demonstrate the tangible impact of our work and to unveil exciting new initiatives. These things have their place, but they can also be distractions or, even worse, idols.

The primary motivation must be love, with all its attendant risks. Sometimes, the wounds of disappointment become so great that we dare not love again. Instead, we construct a protective shell and entrust ourselves no longer to people, or church, or a cause. But this is a less than fully human way of living. To love and to be hurt is of the essence of our humanity.

6 The point of it all

Colossians 1:11–29

Mission is a long-haul endeavour and it is helpful if we maintain a sense of how our story fits into the bigger picture. The bookends of salvation history are represented here by the fact that our salvation is assured (v. 12) because Christ has rescued us (v. 13) and God in Christ has reconciled all things to himself (v. 20)—but we may only see the firstfruits of that reconciliation now, in the places where God's kingdom is already breaking in.

Mission takes place between these twin realities—mission accomplished and mission to be completed. These two dimensions shape the way we approach the task, especially when the weight of ministry threatens to overpower us.

Mission accomplished will give us confidence. We are not responsible for the salvation of the world. The words 'It is finished' (John 19:30) are full of meaning, signifying Jesus' life of perfect obedience to the Father's will, the fulfilment of the law and the bearing of the curse of sin. All of that is accomplished, and the resurrection is the firstfruits of all the glory that is to come (Colossians 1:18). Living in the reality of mission accomplished means that the glory belongs to Christ and not to us.

Mission 'not yet complete' will inspire us to action. Paul speaks of his unceasing prayers for the Christians in Colosse (Colossians 1:3–9), and he assures them that he toils and struggles with all the energy he has, to play his part in bringing the victory of Christ into people's lives (v. 29).

John Bunyan's pilgrim carried the weight of sin on his back until he saw at the cross that he could let go and allow his burden to roll away. In mission, it should never be a burden of guilt or a sense of earning salvation that drives us, nor a messiah complex that usurps the place of the world's true Saviour. What drives us is the love and compassion of Christ, first experienced in our own lives and then reflected into the lives of others. Alongside this love is a passionate commitment to the truth that humankind can experience the fullness of life only in Christ.

Guidelines

Here are seven questions to consider.

- Think of the people who regularly attend your church. Do you think of yourself as deploying each one of them as a missionary into your neighbourhood every week?
- What might it mean for you to be a fusion of 'the person you were, the person you are becoming and the people you have come to serve'?
- Can you think of any times when the gospel is not seen as good news?
- Jesus knew that his life had a higher purpose. Do you have a sense that your story is part of a bigger picture? How would you express that in your own words?
- Can you think of ways in which your church presents the gospel as a multisensory experience?
- In section 5 I wrote that sometimes 'the wounds of disappointment become so great that we dare not love again'. Can you think of times when that has happened or has been a temptation?
- Can you think of examples in your own experience, or that of your church, where you can see the tension between 'mission accomplished' and 'mission not yet completed'?

This page is left blank for your notes.

Guidelines forthcoming issue

DAVID SPRIGGS

Our next issue of *Guidelines*, covering the months of January to April, includes contributions from three new writers, all introduced below.

It is hard to avoid the contribution that the physical context makes to the biblical story, once it is drawn to our attention. The 'wilderness', for instance, features heavily in that interim time between Israel's leaving Egypt and entering the promised land. So much happens in the wilderness, including the giving of the covenant and the ten commandments at Sinai. The 'wilderness' is also of great significance for Jesus as he faces down the onslaught of Satan there in his temptations.

It is illuminating, then, to explore some of the ways that landscapes have shaped the Bible, under the expert guidance of the Bishop of Dudley, the Rt Revd Graham Usher. His emphasis is on the way landscapes, such as trees, seas, deserts and gardens, have enhanced and mediated people's encounters with God.

It is not a thousand miles away from this to start thinking about Celtic saints. Heather Fenton, who will be well known to many of you as Editor of *The Reader*, shares some of her reflections on St Patrick, St David and St Columba. Their locations had a profound impact on them, and they in turn influenced their locations, not only during their lifetimes but for centuries afterward. However, the primary focus for Heather is on six psalms that echo aspects of these saints' experiences. This is a richly evocative and illuminating process.

Finally I want to draw your attention to C.L. Crouch and her two weeks of notes on the book of Micah. Although Micah is probably less well loved than Amos and Hosea, two of the other twelve 'minor prophets', he provides us with fascinating insights into the journey of faith (and sometimes 'unfaith') that God's people took. The book contains some very well-known passages, such as the promise of a future ruler from Bethlehem (5:2), the amazing passage extolling justice and mercy above sacrifice (6:6–8) and the intriguing prophecy that many nations will say, 'Come, let us go up to the mountain of the Lord, to the house of the God of Jacob, that he may teach us his ways, and that we may walk in his paths' (4:2)—intriguing because it appears almost identically in Isaiah 2:3.

Carly Crouch shows us, though, that this book contains more riches than just these passages. She provides us with penetrating insights not only into the message of Micah ('the book's concern with justice strikes a consistent note throughout') but also into the way this prophetic word went on speaking to God's people over centuries to come and can continue to do so today.

These are just three of the great contributions we have ready for our next issue. I'm sure you won't want to miss them, and please encourage your friends to join as readers of *Guidelines* too.

Author profile: David Kerrigan

Here we introduce Revd David Kerrigan, who has written for us on 'Mission and incarnation' in this issue. We can look forward to further notes from David in the January–April 2017 issue, on 'Mission and the cross' and 'Mission and resurrection'. David writes:

Growing up, Alan Whicker was my hero! If you don't know who Alan Whicker is, you're probably aged under 40, so I will only say that he was the first TV-age travel celebrity. Week after week he roamed the globe and sowed in me the seeds of curiosity for our amazing world and its peoples.

The home in which I watched *Whicker's World* was a Christian home and I attended church regularly from the week I was born, but nothing prepared me for the moment in my early 20s when God revealed himself to me afresh. It was a process that happened over some months but it came to a head one evening, talking to two wonderful older Christians at the kitchen table. As they were preparing to leave, I said, 'The only thing I fear now is that I might lose the faith I've found.' They sat back down and opened up Ephesians 2:8: 'It is by grace you have been saved, through faith—and this is not from yourselves, it is the gift of God.' The last piece of the picture was complete. God's word spoke to me, not for the first time, nor the last.

Put these two things together and you'll realise why, soon after we were married, my wife and I were challenged to become missionaries. The Baptist Missionary Society (today 'BMS World Mission') received our call and within 18 months Janet and I, and two small children, were on our way to Bangladesh. Our travelling years had started!

I was business manager of a general and leprosy hospital and Janet, a nurse-midwife, worked part time in our Under 5s clinic. We learnt Bengali and I started to preach and teach. In later years I studied at Spurgeon's College in London. I was a pastor in Exeter before we went to live in Sri Lanka, where I served as BMS Asia Team Leader, now with two teenage children. In those years I had the privilege of becoming President of United Mission to Nepal, made a first BMS visit to Afghanistan (then still under the Taliban) and opened our work there. We returned to the UK in 1999, where I've been involved in BMS leadership since.

Over these years my faith has been hugely shaped by that single verse, Ephesians 2:8. It remains my touchstone: 'by grace you have been saved, though faith...' For me, the gospel must always be a message of grace or we have gone astray.

Today I've had the privilege of travelling to more than 70 countries. In each one, God's people find themselves in boundary places where belief and unbelief meet, where a Christian worldview encounters a non-Christian worldview. If this concept isn't clear, just think of how the Bible locates your life in the story that began in Eden, moving through the calling of a chosen people, the life of Christ and the promise of eternity to come. That story shapes how we see the world. So does our Christian understanding of God as a Father who loves us and longs to welcome us home. Billions of people do not know that their life is part of that story, do not know God as a loving Father, and perhaps do not know there is a God at all. All of this is our gift through God's self-revelation in scripture. Without the Bible, we'd be groping in the dark.

I have always seen my primary calling to be a missionary in those boundary places, whether at home or overseas. It's easier to see the boundaries in countries where language, faith and culture bear little resemblance to ours, but they exist just as much in our own locality.

In our Western world, the boundary places for us can be religious, technological, medical, social, economic or political. It is only by having a deep and prayerful engagement with scripture that we will be equipped to bring a Christian perspective to these critical debates.

Today we are wrestling with the ethics of military engagement, and how to respond to millions of refugees and migrants risking life and limb to secure safety and a better life. People are grappling with issues of sexuality and reproductive ethics, including debates about the 'right to life' versus 'the right to choose' at the beginning and end of our human journey. In all these things, knowing the heart of scripture is to know the heartbeat of God.

I pray that God will give each of us the opportunity to be an effective missionary presence in our boundary places. I pray too that *Guidelines* will be a source of deep enrichment for the task in hand.

Recommended reading

ESTHER TAYLOR

Lighted Windows
An Advent calendar for a world in waiting

MARGARET SILF

pb, 9780857464323, £7.99

From the bestselling author Margaret Silf, *Lighted Windows* (revised and updated since its first edition in 2002) offers readings, reflections and prayers or points for meditation for every day from 1 December to 6 January (Epiphany). The book is based on the theme of looking through the 'windows' of human experience to discover more about God and his call to men and women to follow him. It is also a testimony to the power of waiting—as people wait for Christmas through the Advent season, and as the birth of Messiah was awaited through the centuries. Waiting can be difficult at times, but Christmas proves the value of patience and of taking time to stop, to look out, to listen.

Margaret Silf is an ecumenical Christian, committed to working across and beyond the denominational divides. After working in the computer industry, she left to devote herself to writing in the area of Christian spirituality. Her previous books include *Landmarks: An Ignatian journey*, *Taste and See: Adventuring into prayer*, *Wayfaring: A gospel journey into life* (all published by DLT) and *Sacred Spaces: Stations on a Celtic way* (Lion).

To read an extract from *Lighted Windows*, please turn to page 145.

Heaven's Morning
Rethinking the destination

DAVID WINTER

pb, 9780857464767, £7.99

The Bible, especially the New Testament, has plenty to say about resurrection and heaven, but what does it actually mean in practice? David Winter's *Heaven's Morning* explores the biblical teaching on what happens after death and considers what difference this can make to our lives, day by day. Winter, one of the UK's most celebrated Christian authors, proves that eternity can be an empowering source of hope to our sceptical, anxious world, and clarifies what is waiting for us—just beyond.

David Winter is one of the UK's most popular and long established Christian writers and broadcasters. He has written many books over the last 60 years, including *At the End of the Day*, *Facing the Darkness*, *Finding the Light* and *Journey to Jerusalem* for BRF. He also writes for *New Daylight* and contributed regularly to Radio 4's *Thought for the Day* from 1989 to 2012.

St Aidan's Way of Mission
Celtic insights for a post-Christian world

RAY SIMPSON with BRENT LYONS-LEE

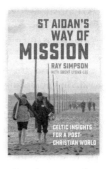

pb, 9780857464859, £7.99

Surveying the life and times of Aidan of Lindisfarne, this book brings great insight not only into the character of this complex Celtic man but also into missional approaches that can inspire outreach and discipleship for today's church. As in his previous BRF book, *Hilda of Whitby*, Ray Simpson shows that such figures from past centuries can provide models for Christian life and witness today. Combining historical fact and spiritual teaching, he introduces St Aidan more fully than ever before.

Revd Ray Simpson is a founder of the international new monastic movement known as The Community of Aidan and Hilda and is principal tutor of its Celtic Christian Studies programmes. He has written more than 30 books on spirituality and lives on Lindisfarne, offering a ministry of counsel and support to visitors, especially those in church leadership. He leads retreats on several continents.

Revd Brent Lyons-Lee contributes material from an Australian cross-cultural mission perspective. He is part of the Baptist Union Mission Catalyst team (Victoria, Australia) and a member of The Community of Aidan and Hilda, and has co-written with Ray a book that explores indigenous mission in Australia: *Celtic Spirituality in an Australian Landscape* (St Aidan Press).

Confidence in the Living God
David and Goliath revisited

ANDREW WATSON

pb, 9780857464828, £7.99

Confidence lies at the heart of society, determining the success or failure of the economy, the government, schools, churches and individuals. As Christians, we are called to proclaim our faith in God, but how can we maintain this confidence in an increasingly secularised culture where faith is often seen as marginal, embarrassing or even downright dangerous?

Using the story of David and Goliath as his starting point, Andrew Watson shows how the Lord can indeed be our confidence, whatever the odds. The book includes a discussion guide and is ideal as a whole-church course on the subject of confidence.

Andrew Watson is Bishop of Guildford and author of *The Fourfold Leadership of Jesus* and *The Way of the Desert*, a BRF Lent book. He was previously Bishop of Aston and vicar of St Stephen's, East Twickenham, where he helped pioneer three church plants.

To order a copy of any of these books, please use the order form on pages 149–150. BRF books are also available from your local Christian bookshop or from **www.brfonline.org.uk**.

An extract from
Lighted Windows

The following extracts from BRF's Advent book for
2016, by **Margaret Silf**, are from the Introduction and
the reading for 5 December, entitled 'Answer books'.

Introduction

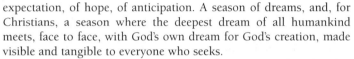

The First of December, and Christmas is
just around the corner! It's the season of
expectation, of hope, of anticipation. A season of dreams, and, for
Christians, a season where the deepest dream of all humankind
meets, face to face, with God's own dream for God's creation, made
visible and tangible to everyone who seeks.

One of my most abiding memories is of an evening shared with a
friend who had experienced a particularly traumatic childhood. We
were talking about our favourite fairy stories, and she told me... of
how much the story of 'The Little Matchgirl' had come to mean for
her, not just in her dreams but in her Christian journeying too.

As she retold the story, it came to life in a way that reflects, for me,
something of the spirit of this Advent journey. The little matchgirl
was a young child, undernourished and very poor. She earned her
daily bread by selling matches, but the earnings were sparse, and at
home a cruel father was waiting to punish her if she failed to bring
home enough money. One dark winter night she was standing in her
usual place, shivering, and gazing at the lighted windows of the big
houses all around her, catching fleeting glimpses of all that was going
on inside those rooms—the preparations for Christmas, the lovely
gifts, the bright decorations, the happy faces, the smell of Christmas
puddings and roasting goose.

All she had was a box of matches... 'Dare I strike one?' she
wondered. She took out a match, and struck it, gazing for a few
brief moments into its blaze of light. As she did so, she imagined
that it was one of those lighted windows. She looked inside, in her
imagination, and entered into a warm room where loving friends
might welcome her. Another match; another scene. Another window
to look into. Perhaps a fine dinner set out for a family. The crackling

of the goose, the aroma of mince pies. Food and shelter. And so she continued, until she came to the last match in the box.

The story has a bittersweet ending. As she strikes her last match, the little matchgirl sees a shooting star falling across the night sky, and her granny is standing there, smiling, waiting to gather the child into her arms and carry her home to heaven. The frozen child is discovered the next morning, with an empty matchbox in her hands and a deep, contented smile across her white face.

This Advent journey invites you to share something of the magic and mystery of what it means to look into some of your own 'lighted windows'... During the first three weeks of the journey, we look, day by day, into a series of windows opening up into glimpses of how we might discover God's guidance in our lives, how we might become more trusting of that guidance, and how we might catch something of God's wisdom. During Christmas week, the 'windows' open wide, inviting us to enter the heart of the mystery of God's coming to earth. And as the journey moves on through to the turning of the year, and the feast of the Epiphany, the windows turn into doors, through which we are sent out again into a world that is waiting—and longing—for the touch of God's love upon its broken heart.

Answer books

For surely I know the plans I have for you, says the Lord, plans for your welfare and not for harm, to give you a future with hope. Then when you call upon me and come and pray to me, I will hear you. When you search for me, you will find me; if you seek me with all your heart, I will let you find me, says the Lord, and I will restore your fortunes and gather you from all the nations and all the places where I have driven you, says the Lord, and I will bring you back to the place from which I sent you into exile...

But this is the covenant that I will make with the house of Israel after those days, says the Lord: I will put my law within them, and I will write it on their hearts; and I will be their God, and they shall be my people. No longer shall they teach one another, or say to each other, 'Know the Lord', for they shall all know me, from the least of them to the greatest, says the Lord; for I will forgive their iniquity, and remember their sin no more.

JEREMIAH 29:11–14; 31:33–34 (NRSV)

Perhaps you have heard the story of the schoolboy who dreamed of becoming a mathematician. This same lad also liked to be out on the town in the evenings, and he often skipped his homework. When this happened, he would hastily throw his exercises together on the bus the next morning by looking at the answers at the end of the book.

One day his teacher took him to one side and told him just one simple truth: 'You will never become a mathematician by looking up the answers to the problems in the back of the book,' he said, 'even though, ironically, those answers will usually be the right ones.'

Perhaps this wisdom is something of what lies behind the game of hide-and-seek that God appears to be playing with us so often. 'Come on,' God urges us, 'come and look for me. Where have I hidden myself today?'

'Is this game God's idea of fun?' we might be forgiven for wondering. Or is it, rather, God's way of teaching our hearts divine meanings and sacred ways? We might almost hear God whispering, very gently, 'You will never become fully the person I created you to be by cribbing life's answers from creeds and doctrines, even though these doctrines may well be right and true. You will only become your true self by working through for yourself the challenges that life presents.'

A daunting prospect! But from Jeremiah's words today we discover that we are not alone in the task. God has promised to plant the holy law deep within our own hearts. So does this mean that we have some kind of 'answer book' inside us, if we only knew how to access it? I think not, much as we might wish it were so! God's answers don't come ready-made. They have to be discovered. And the prophet goes on to give us a clue about this process of discovery.

This 'law' that God has planted in our hearts, it seems, is more like the bond of a personal relationship than the terms of an equation. It is a sense of alignment between our own hearts and the heart of God that will deepen and strengthen every time we use it, so that gradually, step by step, we will learn to recognise when we are acting out of our truest centre, and when we are slipping off-course. The closer we come to this kind of discernment, the less we will need human guides and teachers.

The giving of God's guidance is something organic and alive. God plants it in our hearts, and writes it for each of us uniquely, and then gives it growth, until it bears the fruits of God's kingdom. It is a guidance that leads to right relationship—a mutuality of relationship between God and all God's people. It can't be copied from the back of the book. It has to be lived! It is a journey of discovery, not a system of salvation.

Jeremiah gives us two further clues about the nature of this mysterious 'law' in our hearts:

- It reflects the very dynamic of the holy, always to bring good out of bad, better out of good, and best out of better. The dynamic of evil works the other way round, always diminishing our good to mediocre, and our poor to worst. Observing how these contradictory movements are working in us at any particular moment is an important tool for cooperating with God's 'law'.
- It is for all God's people, not just for those who understand the rules of 'discernment'. It flows from God's own presence deep within our hearts, and that presence is often more obvious in those who are not overburdened with their own 'achievements'.

There is a beautiful story of how, one day, God was talking with the angels about where to hide within creation, so that humankind might not find God too easily but might grow through their searching.

The first angel suggested the depths of the earth as a hiding place. 'No,' said God. 'They will soon learn to dig mines, and they will find me too soon.'

'What about hiding on their moon?' the second angel suggested. 'No,' said God. 'It won't be long before they reach the moon with their technology. They will find me too soon.'

It was the third angel who hit on the Great Idea. 'Why don't you hide yourself in their own hearts?' she suggested. 'They'll never think to look there.' So God did just that, and this is why it takes us so long to find God, step by step as we do our living. And that, in turn, is what makes us grow.

You might like to ask God today to draw you a little closer to the secret depths of your own heart, where the secret of the holy is hidden, for you to discover.

Lord, give me the courage to go beyond my ready-made answers and to know you, rather than merely knowing about you. Amen

BRF PUBLICATIONS ORDER FORM

To order our resources online, please visit **www.brfonline.org.uk**

Please send me the following book(s):	Quantity	Price	Total
432 3 **Lighted Windows** Margaret Silf	_____	£7.99	_____
500 9 **Could This Be God?** Brian Harris	_____	£9.99	_____
524 5 **Quiet Spaces Prayer Journal**	_____	£9.99	_____
476 7 **Heaven's Morning** David Winter	_____	£7.99	_____
485 9 **St Aidan's Way of Mission** Ray Simpson	_____	£7.99	_____
482 8 **Confidence in the Living God** Andrew Watson	_____	£7.99	_____
Quiet Spaces FREE sample copy	_____	£0.00	_____

Total cost of books £ _____

Donation £ _____

Postage and packing (*see overleaf*) £ _____

TOTAL £ _____

Account no. _____

Title _____ First name/initials _____ Surname _____

Address _____

_____ Postcode _____

Telephone _____ Email _____

Total enclosed £ _____ (cheques should be made payable to 'BRF')

Please charge my Mastercard ☐ Visa ☐ Debit card ☐ with £ _____

Card no. ☐☐☐☐ ☐☐☐☐ ☐☐☐☐ ☐☐☐☐

Valid from ☐☐ ☐☐ Expires ☐☐ ☐☐

Security code* ☐☐☐ *Last 3 digits on the reverse of the card
ESSENTIAL IN ORDER TO PROCESS YOUR ORDER

Signature _____ Date ____ / ____ / ____

(*essential if paying by credit card*)

*To read our terms and find out about cancelling your order,
please visit www.brfonline.org.uk/terms*

Please send your completed form with the appropriate payment to:
BRF, 15 The Chambers, Vineyard, Abingdon OX14 3FE

The Bible Reading Fellowship (BRF) is a Registered Charity (233280). VAT No: GB 238 5574 35

POSTAGE AND PACKING CHARGES			
Order value	UK	Europe	Rest of World
Under £7.00	£1.25	£3.00	£5.50
£7.00–£29.99	£2.25	£5.50	£10.00
£30.00 & over	FREE	Prices on request	

Transforming Lives and Communities

BRF is a charity that is passionate about making a difference through the Christian faith. We want to see lives and communities transformed through our creative programmes and resources for individuals, churches and schools. We are doing this by resourcing:

- **Christian growth and understanding of the Bible.** Through our Bible reading notes, books, digital resources, Quiet Days and other events, we're resourcing individuals, groups and leaders in churches for their own spiritual journey and for their ministry.

- **Church outreach in the local community.** BRF is the home of three programmes that churches are embracing to great effect as they seek to engage with their local communities: Messy Church, Who Let The Dads Out? and The Gift of Years.

- **Teaching Christianity in primary schools.** Our Barnabas in Schools team is working with primary-aged children and their teachers, enabling them to explore Christianity creatively within the school curriculum.

- **Children's and family ministry.** Through our Barnabas in Churches and Faith in Homes websites and published resources, we're working with churches and families, enabling children under 11, and the adults working with them, to explore Christianity creatively and bring the Bible alive.

Do you share our vision?

Sales of our books and Bible reading notes cover the cost of producing them. However, our other programmes are funded primarily by donations, grants and legacies. If you share our vision, would you help us to transform even more lives and communities? Your prayers and financial support are vital for the work that we do.

- You could support BRF's ministry with a one-off gift or regular donation (using the response form on page 153 or 154).
- You could consider making a bequest to BRF in your will (page 152).
- You could encourage your church to support BRF as part of your church's giving to home mission—perhaps focusing on a specific area of our ministry, or a particular member of our Barnabas team.
- Most important of all, you could support BRF with your prayers.

The difference a gift in your Will can make

 Gifts left in Wills don't need to be huge to help us make a real difference, and for every £1 you give, we will invest 88p back into charitable activities.

BRF's vision is to see lives and communities transformed through the Christian faith. For over 90 years we have been able to do amazing things thanks to the generosity of those who have supported us during their lifetime and through gifts in wills.

One of the fastest growing areas of our work is Messy Church. Messy Church reaches people of all ages who have often never set foot in a church before, by being 'church' differently. It is being delivered in a variety of contexts in local communities, including care homes, prisons and schools, in inner city and rural areas. Week by week we are seeing new Messy Churches starting up across the UK and around the globe, and across all major church denominations. We estimate that over 500,000 people are attending Messy Church each month.

A gift in your will could help fund the growth, development and sustainability of programmes like BRF's Messy Church for many years to come. Just imagine what we could do over the next 90 years with your help.

For further information about making a gift to BRF in your will, please contact Sophie Aldred on 01865 319700 or email fundraising@brf.org.uk.

Whatever you can do or give, we thank you for your support.

SHARING OUR VISION – MAKING A GIFT

I would like to make a gift to support BRF. Please use my gift for:

☐ where it is needed most ☐ Barnabas Children's Ministry
☐ Messy Church ☐ Who Let The Dads Out? ☐ The Gift of Years

Title	First name/initials	Surname

Address

	Postcode

Email

Telephone	Date

giftaid it **You can add an extra 25p to every £1 you give.**

Please treat as Gift Aid donations all qualifying gifts of money made

☐ today, ☐ in the past four years, ☐ and in the future.

I am a UK taxpayer and understand that if I pay less Income Tax and/or Capital Gains Tax in the current tax year than the amount of Gift Aid claimed on all my donations, it is my responsibility to pay any difference.

☐ My donation does not qualify for Gift Aid.

Please notify BRF if you want to cancel this Gift Aid declaration, change your name or address, or you no longer pay sufficient tax on your income and/or capital gains

Please complete other side of form ➡

Please return to:
BRF, 15 The Chambers, Vineyard, Abingdon OX14 3FE

The Bible Reading Fellowship (BRF) is a Registered Charity (No. 233280)

SHARING OUR VISION – MAKING A GIFT

Regular Giving

By Direct Debit:

☐ I would like to make a regular gift of £ [   ] per month/quarter/year.
Please also complete the Direct Debit instruction on page 159.

By Standing Order:

Please contact Priscilla Kew, tel. 01235 462305; priscilla.kew@brf.org.uk

One-off Donation

Please accept my gift of:

☐ £10 ☐ £50 ☐ £100 Other £ [   ]

by (*delete as appropriate*):

☐ Cheque/Charity Voucher payable to 'BRF'

☐ Mastercard/Visa/Debit card/Charity Card

Name on card

Card no. [ ][ ][ ][ ] [ ][ ][ ][ ] [ ][ ][ ][ ] [ ][ ][ ][ ]

Valid from [M][M][Y][Y] Expires [M][M][Y][Y]

Security code* [ ][ ][ ]   *Last 3 digits on the reverse of the card
ESSENTIAL IN ORDER TO PROCESS THE PAYMENT

Signature | Date

We like to acknowledge all donations. However, if you do not wish to receive an acknowledgement, please tick here ☐

↶ Please complete other side of form

Please return to:
BRF, 15 The Chambers, Vineyard, Abingdon OX14 3FE

The Bible Reading Fellowship (BRF) is a Registered Charity (233280). VAT No: GB 238 5574 35

GL0316

How to encourage Bible reading in your church

BRF has been helping individuals connect with the Bible for over 90 years. We want to support churches as they seek to encourage church members into regular Bible reading.

Order a Bible reading resources pack

This pack is designed to give your church the tools to publicise our Bible reading notes. It includes:

• Sample Bible reading notes for your congregation to try.

• Publicity resources, including a poster.

• A church magazine feature about Bible reading notes.

The pack is free, but we welcome a £5 donation to cover the cost of postage. If you require a pack to be sent outside the UK or require a specific number of sample Bible reading notes, please contact us for postage costs. More information about what the current pack contains is available on our website.

How to order and find out more

• Visit www.biblereadingnotes.org.uk/for-churches

• Telephone BRF on 01865 319700 between 9.15 am and 5.30 pm

• Write to us at BRF, 15 The Chambers, Vineyard, Abingdon OX14 3FE

Keep informed about our latest initiatives

We are continuing to develop resources to help churches encourage people into regular Bible reading, wherever they are on their journey. Join our email list at www.biblereadingnotes.org.uk/helpingchurches to stay informed about the latest initiatives that your church could benefit from.

Introduce a friend to our notes

We can send information about our notes and current prices for you to pass on. Please contact us.

GUIDELINES INDIVIDUAL SUBSCRIPTION FORM

All our Bible reading notes can be ordered online by visiting
www.biblereadingnotes.org.uk/subscriptions

☐ I would like to take out a subscription:

Title _____ First name/initials _____ Surname _____

Address _____

_____ Postcode _____

Telephone _____ Email _____

Please send Guidelines beginning with the January 2017 / May 2017 / September 2017 issue (*delete as appropriate*):

(*please tick box*)	UK	Europe	Rest of World
Guidelines	☐ £16.35	☐ £24.90	☐ £28.20
Guidelines 3-year subscription	☐ £43.20	N/A	N/A

Total enclosed £ _____ (cheques should be made payable to 'BRF')

Please charge my Mastercard ☐ Visa ☐ Debit card ☐ with £ _____

Card no. ☐☐☐☐ ☐☐☐☐ ☐☐☐☐ ☐☐☐☐

Valid from [M][M] [Y][Y] Expires [M][M] [Y][Y]

Security code* ☐☐☐ *Last 3 digits on the reverse of the card
ESSENTIAL IN ORDER TO PROCESS YOUR ORDER

Signature _____ Date ___ / ___ / ___
(*essential if paying by credit card*)

To read our terms and find out about cancelling your order, please visit www.brfonline.org.uk/terms

To set up a Direct Debit, please also complete the Direct Debit instruction on page 159 and return it to BRF with this form.

Please send your completed form with the appropriate payment to:
BRF, 15 The Chambers, Vineyard, Abingdon OX14 3FE

GUIDELINES GIFT SUBSCRIPTION FORM

☐ I would like to give a gift subscription (please provide both names and addresses):

Title _____ First name/initials _____ Surname _____

Address _____

_____ Postcode _____

Telephone _____ Email _____

Gift subscription name _____

Gift subscription address _____

_____ Postcode _____

Gift message (20 words max. or include your own gift card):

_____

_____

Please send **Guidelines** beginning with the January 2017 / May 2017 / September 2017 issue (*delete as appropriate*):

(*please tick box*)	UK	Europe	Rest of World
Guidelines	☐ £16.35	☐ £24.90	☐ £28.20
Guidelines 3-year subscription	☐ £43.20	N/A	N/A

Total enclosed £ _____ (cheques should be made payable to 'BRF')

Please charge my Mastercard ☐ Visa ☐ Debit card ☐ with £ _____

Card no. ☐☐☐☐ ☐☐☐☐ ☐☐☐☐ ☐☐☐☐

Valid from ☐☐☐☐ Expires ☐☐☐☐

Security code* ☐☐☐ *Last 3 digits on the reverse of the card
ESSENTIAL IN ORDER TO PROCESS YOUR ORDER

Signature _____ Date ____ / ____ / ____

(*essential if paying by credit card*)

To read our terms and find out about cancelling your order, please visit www.brfonline.org.uk/terms

To set up a Direct Debit, please also complete the Direct Debit instruction on page 159 and return it to BRF with this form.

Please send your completed form with the appropriate payment to:
BRF, 15 The Chambers, Vineyard, Abingdon OX14 3FE

The Bible Reading Fellowship (BRF) is a Registered Charity (233280). VAT No: GB 238 5574 35

DIRECT DEBIT PAYMENT

You can pay for your annual subscription to our Bible reading notes using Direct Debit. You need only give your bank details once, and the payment is made automatically every year until you cancel it. If you would like to pay by Direct Debit, please use the form opposite, entering your BRF account number under 'Reference'.

You are fully covered by the Direct Debit Guarantee:

The Direct Debit Guarantee

· This Guarantee is offered by all banks and building societies that accept instructions to pay Direct Debits.

· If there are any changes to the amount, date or frequency of your Direct Debit, The Bible Reading Fellowship will notify you 10 working days in advance of your account being debited or as otherwise agreed. If you request The Bible Reading Fellowship to collect a payment, confirmation of the amount and date will be given to you at the time of the request.

· If an error is made in the payment of your Direct Debit, by The Bible Reading Fellowship or your bank or building society, you are entitled to a full and immediate refund of the amount paid from your bank or building society.

· If you receive a refund you are not entitled to, you must pay it back when The Bible Reading Fellowship asks you to.

· You can cancel a Direct Debit at any time by simply contacting your bank or building society. Written confirmation may be required. Please also notify us.

The Bible Reading Fellowship

Instruction to your bank or building society to pay by Direct Debit

Please fill in the whole form using a ballpoint pen and return it to:
BRF, 15 The Chambers, Vineyard, Abingdon OX14 3FE

Service User Number: | 5 | 5 | 8 | 2 | 2 | 9 |

Name and full postal address of your bank or building society

To: The Manager	Bank/Building Society
Address	
	Postcode

Name(s) of account holder(s)

Branch sort code

Bank/Building Society account number

Reference

Instruction to your Bank/Building Society

Please pay The Bible Reading Fellowship Direct Debits from the account detailed in this instruction, subject to the safeguards assured by the Direct Debit Guarantee. I understand that this instruction may remain with The Bible Reading Fellowship and, if so, details will be passed electronically to my bank/building society.

Signature(s)

Banks and Building Societies may not accept Direct Debit instructions for some types of account

This page is for your notes.